BERTHE MORISOT

Frontispiece. Berthe Morisot, *Woman in Black*. 1878. Oil on canvas, 73 × 60 cm. (28¾ × 23½ in.) Dublin, National Gallery of Ireland

BERTHE MORISOT

KATHLEEN ADLER and TAMAR GARB

CORNELL UNIVERSITY PRESS
ITHACA, NEW YORK

To our parents

Hilde and Hugo Adler
Cynthia and Ivor Garb

First published in 1987 by Cornell University Press

Library of Congress Cataloging in Publication Data
Adler, Kathleen.
  Berthe Morisot.

  Bibliography: p.
  Includes index.
  1. Morisot, Berthe, 1841–1895. 2. Painters—France—

Biography. I. Garb, Tamar. II. Title.
ND553.M88A83 1987   759.4 [B]   86–29287
ISBN 0–8014–2053–9

Printed in Great Britain by Hazell, Watson and Viney, Aylesbury

Acknowledgements

We wish to thank Pamela Gerrish Nunn for generously allowing us to borrow her M.A. report, 'Berthe Morisot: 1857–1874' (University College, London, 1976); Charles F. Stuckey, of the National Gallery of Art, Washington D.C., for his courteous responses to our queries; our editor, Penelope Marcus; and John House, for his willingness to engage in discussion and his helpful comments on a draft of this text.

Photographic Acknowledgements

Courtesy Museum of Fine Arts, Boston 74; Courtesy of the Harvard University Art Museums (The Fogg Art Museum, Cambridge) Grenville L. Winthrop Bequest 81; © The Art Institute of Chicago. All Rights Reserved 18, 47; National Galleries of Scotland, Edinburgh 63; Reproduced by Courtesy of the Trustees of the British Museum 24, 25, 28, 70, 79; Christie's Colour Library 15; Witt Library, Courtauld Institute 50; Reproduced by Courtesy of the Trustees of the National Gallery, London 12, 39, 98; Photo Claude O'Sughrue, Montpellier 43; All Rights Reserved, The Metropolitan Museum of Art 20, 97; Wildenstein & Co. New York 56; Atelier 53 Paris 1, 67; Photo Bulloz, Paris 34, 65, 71; Giraudon, Paris 11, 17, 23, 26, 30, 36, 55, 66, 89; Studio Lourmel, Photo Routhier, Paris 37, 69, 77; Cliché des Musées Nationaux, Paris 5, 9, 19, 31, 32, 53, 57, 60, 64, 72, 78, 82; Cliché Musées de la Ville de Paris © SPADEM 1987 93.

Contents

1. Berthe Morisot. *Thatched Cottage in Normandy*. 1865. Oil on canvas, 46 × 55 cm. (18 × 21 in.) Paris, Private collection

Preface

Little has been written in English on the work of the nineteenth-century French painter Berthe Morisot, and there is no publication to date which attempts to place her practice within the context of the artistic debates of her time or the situation which she as an upper-middle-class woman must have faced. In standard accounts of Impressionism, Morisot is accorded a marginal place and her work is most often viewed in relation to that of her male colleagues rather than in its own right. Where they do exist, many recent accounts of her work perpetuate the predominantly nineteenth-century stereotypical view of her work as the unmediated expression of an intrinsic femininity, delicate and charming in nature, but essentially lightweight and insignificant when compared with the work of her male contemporaries.

In this book we hope to redress some of the imbalances and inaccuracies which have dogged accounts of Morisot's work. By breaking with the customary chronological sequence of the monograph, and by focusing, in each of the five chapters in the book, on an issue relevant to the work that she produced and the time in which she lived, we hope to give the reader an understanding of what it was like to be a woman artist in nineteenth-century France, what it was like to be a woman of Morisot's class during this time, and how she reconciled the private world of the 'feminine sphere' with the public world of artistic practice.

Chapter one considers Morisot's education and background, describing her move beyond the accepted idea of painting as a suitable accomplishment for upper-middle-class women and indicating how her wealth and social position facilitated a private artistic education. In the second chapter we discuss Morisot's contacts with other artists so as to locate her practice within a highly specific artistic context and to dispel the popular notion that she painted as she did because this was a natural way for a woman to paint. Discussion of her contacts and context testifies to her participation in the artistic debates of her time. In chapter three we examine her relationship with Impressionist painters, her involvement in the independent group exhibitions, and her part in the formation of the way of working which has come to be known as 'Impressionist'. We consider the implications of her identity as a woman for the way that her work was perceived by contemporary critics. In chapter four we discuss Baudelaire's exhortation to painters to turn to the representation of modern life subjects and the connotations this had for a woman painter of Morisot's class, and in chapter five we look at Morisot's picturing of place, considering her relationship to suburban Passy and the environs of Paris, as well as to the resorts in which she spent the summer months.

Although each one of the following chapters deals with a separate issue and the book may be read as a collection of five essays with Morisot as their focus, the central theme which runs throughout each of the chapters is the issue of Morisot's identity as a woman. This book seeks to make explicit, to spell out and explore, the situation which a woman who wished to become a professional painter at this time might have faced. We demonstrate how Morisot's gender established certain constraints on her movements, determined to some extent her subject matter, mediated her relationships with her colleagues, and affected her critics' perceptions of her work. We have entered into this project firm in the belief that no adequate account of Morisot's production can be made without highlighting the fact that she was a woman and without examining the significance of this for her work and the way that it has been seen historically.

1 *Setting the Scene*

There was little in Berthe Morisot's background and upbringing to suggest that she was to commit herself to the life of a serious painter. Her own family belonged to the wealthy and cultured *haut bourgeois*; her father was a government administrator, although he had studied architecture at the École des Beaux Arts, but there was no precedent in her immediate family for a professional commitment to art. In such families, art had a particularly circumscribed role; its function was seen to lie in uplifting, in ennobling and transforming the individual. Through it, the *haute bourgeoisie* could differentiate itself from what it saw as the vulgarity of the burgeoning middle or commercial classes. Art functioned as the marker of taste, of sensibility, of 'difference'. It was created by men of 'genius' and appreciated by men of taste.

Nor did Morisot come from a family in which women had broken the boundaries of convention. Her mother Marie-Joséphine Cornélie Morisot, born Thomas, although of the same class as her husband, had, as a girl, not had access to the same formal education as he. She was accomplished in those areas which were deemed appropriate for a woman of her class, having a smattering of education and a pleasant manner. Morisot described her mother as 'well read and sociable, and an agreeable companion; she had the gift of pleasing people, and an amiable disposition'. Her recollections of her grandmother, Marie-Caroline Maynial, demonstrate the limits placed on women's education at the time: 'Her education at Saint Denis, which was at that time regarded as superior, had given her, besides facility in French, which she wrote most correctly, scattered notions of ancient history and some rudiments of science. But her mind went no further: she firmly believed that this was the apogee of female intellectual development . . .'

Morisot's grandmother was not alone in her views. Born in 1841 in Bourges, Morisot lived in a time when art, culture, and scientific knowledge were widely regarded as the province of men. The spheres of masculine and feminine activity were carefully delineated and based on fixed notions of appropriate masculine and feminine behaviour. Nowhere were the debates on 'women's nature' more clearly stated than in the ongoing arguments on women's education which continued throughout the century. Most public statements on education argued for a separate and different schooling for boys and girls, based not only on their different natures but on their concomitant social roles. While boys needed to be prepared for leadership, the pursuit of excellence, and public service, girls were to be groomed for a life of domestic responsibility, motherhood, appropriate subservience, piety, and gentle accomplishment in those arts deemed suitable, such as needlework, watercolour, and singing—*les arts des femmes.*

Within such a world view, the professional artist could only conceivably be male. Well into this century, to be a woman artist has been in itself widely regarded as at best unfortunate, at worst, unnatural. The most extreme exponents of this view asserted that women who created art or pursued learning were not 'true' women. They had, of necessity, therefore to be considered to be men. The adjective 'masculine' was widely applied to women artists and writers of the period and those women who did possess skill and strength in their work were sometimes literally called men, thought to be copying men, or accused of using men to do their work. When one of Marie Bashkirtseff's works was regarded by the male students at the Académie Julian at which she was a student as 'powerful, even brutal . . .' they declared it to be 'the work of a young man'. The practice of prominent women writers or artists, like George Sand or Rosa Bonheur, of wearing men's clothing must have been seen to confirm this idea, and both these women were ridiculed for their manner of dressing. A contemporary caricature captures the horrified reaction of the male spectator to an exhibition in the early 1880s devoted solely to the work of women artists, while in the distance a suitably socialized and fashionably dressed woman parades on the arm of her male escort.

What was considered appropriate was that women be accomplished amateurs, that they create suitably pretty artefacts for use or decoration within the home. Important here was needlework, which was widely regarded in the nineteenth century not only as the product of a particularly female sensibility but also as instrumental in inculcating a set of proper 'feminine' attitudes and ways of behaviour. Painting in oils and watercolour became increasingly valued as useful female accomplishments but the state art school, the École des Beaux Arts, remained closed to women until 1897 and even then was only opened after a long and vociferous struggle led by prominent women artists. Drawing had long been considered an important part of girls' education, and Jean-Jacques Rousseau had included it in his prescriptions for girls in his influential book *Émile*, published in 1762. State-run design schools were open to women as it was thought that working-class women could make a useful contribution to the areas of fashion, home decoration, and industrial design. By 1869 there were seven schools of design for men in Paris but as many as twenty for women.

Morisot's beginnings in art can be linked to the idea of 'accomplishment'. Her earliest education had been entrusted to an English governess, and, like most girls of her class, she received her early schooling in the home. State educational

2. Joseph Benoît Guichard. *Night of the Orgy.* c. 1833. Oil on canvas, 45 × 53 cm. (17¾ × 20⅞ in.) Lyons, Musée des Beaux Arts

provision for girls was minimal at this time. She was encouraged to appreciate literature, to draw, and to make clay models, and was sent to piano lessons. Morisot and her two sisters Yves and Edma were later sent to an exclusive private school in Passy after the family had moved to Paris in 1855. When Morisot was sixteen, her mother thought it appropriate that the three daughters should be given art lessons so that they could each give their father a drawing as a birthday gift. She chose Geoffrey Alphonse Chocarne, an academic painter, as their instructor. At this stage Mme Morisot could not have believed that any of her daughters would become serious painters. They submitted themselves to Chocarne's arduous instruction, based on the widely accepted belief that drawing was the basis of all learning in art. 'His teaching began with lessons on crosshatch. Crosshatch with straight strokes for plane surfaces, or with curved strokes for convex or concave surfaces, very compact crosshatch for shadows, less

3. Edgar Degas. *Mary Cassatt at the Louvre*. 1879–80. Drypoint. 43 × 30.6 cm. (16⅞ × 12 in.) (sheet) Cleveland, Museum of Art, the Charles W. Harkness Endowment Fund

4. Winslow Homer. *Art Students and Copyists in the Louvre*. 1867. Wood engraving. *Harper's Weekly*, 11 January 1868

close for half-shadows, and very loose for chiaroscuro.' After only four such exacting lessons Yves proclaimed her lack of interest but Berthe and Edma were not as easily deterred and determined to find another teacher. Mme Morisot knew of Joseph-Benoît Guichard through his wife who ran a school for girls in the Rue des Moulins, close to the Morisots' home, and the two sisters became his pupils.

Guichard was then in his fifties. He was a follower of both Ingres and Delacroix and had shown regularly at the Paris Salons from the 1830s (Pl. 2). He was a gifted teacher and it was he who first detected the ability of the Morisot sisters. Guichard was particularly interested in the education of girls. From 1868 until his death in 1880 he was to direct a municipal course in drawing and painting for girls in Lyons, where he became director of the École des Beaux Arts. Berthe and Edma returned from their first lesson with him filled with enthusiasm. He had discussed the importance of tonal values with them and asked them to prepare a sketch containing a white accent for the next lesson. Berthe executed a small pastel landscape with a flock of sheep. Other lessons involved making sepia copies from reproductions of Gavarni drawings which M. Morisot owned. Copying 'from the flat' was a standard art educational practice.

This was combined with the traditional drawing from plaster casts, 'from the round', and working from nature. The sisters executed *plein-air* sketches in the summer under Guichard's guidance but such works were regarded exclusively as preparatory to work to be done in the studio. Guichard soon found it necessary to warn Mme Morisot of the seriousness of his pupils' involvement with art. According to Tiburce, the sisters' younger brother, Guichard was almost frightened by his discovery of their talent. 'Considering the character of your daughters,' he told their mother, 'my teaching will not endow them with minor drawing room accomplishments; they will become painters. Do you realize what this means? In the upper-class milieu to which you belong, this will be revolutionary, I might almost say catastrophic. Are you sure that you will not come to curse the day when art, having gained admission to your home, now so respectable and peaceful, will become the sole arbiter of the fate of two of your children?' Guichard's fears emerged from a widespread nineteenth-century suspicion of the notion of the female professional. Throughout her life Morisot

5. Camille Corot. *View of Tivoli.* 1843. Oil on canvas, 43.5 × 60.5 cm. (17.4 × 24.2 in.) Paris, Musée du Louvre

6. Edma Morisot.
*Portrait of Berthe
Morisot.* 1863. Oil
on canvas, Paris,
Private collection

was to be undermined repeatedly as a professional painter because she was a woman, and Théodore Duret, author of one of the earliest texts on Impressionism, commented that she was secretly hurt at being regarded as an amateur.

Mme Morisot was not deterred by Guichard's warning and from this time on was to remain a constant, although not uncritical, support to her daughters, especially Berthe. Having realized the seriousness of his pupils' involvement and having gained their mother's approval, Guichard's next step was to introduce them to the practice of copying from Old Masters in the Louvre. Mme Morisot's support is shown by her willingness to accompany her daughters as a chaperone. It would have been unseemly for young women of their class to venture out unaccompanied and Mme Morisot sat knitting while her daughters worked. The naturalist painter Marie Bashkirtseff was later to express her frustration with the inhibition of movement the requirement of a chaperone necessitated. In a journal entry of January 1879, she wrote:

> What I long for is the freedom of going about alone, of coming and going, of sitting in the seats of the Tuileries, and especially in the Luxembourg, of stopping and looking at the artistic shops, of entering churches and museums, of walking about the old streets at night; that's what I long for; and that's the freedom without which one cannot become a real artist. Do you imagine that I get much good from what I see, chaperoned as I am, and when, in order to go to the Louvre, I must wait for my carriage, my lady companion and family? ... This is one of the principal reasons why there are no female artists.

Notwithstanding such inhibiting factors, many women copied in the Louvre in the nineteenth century. Working from the 'Old Masters' was regarded as essential for the education of any aspiring artist. It was in the galleries of the Louvre that Degas situated his series of studies of the artist Mary Cassatt (Pl. 3). Morisot herself was first registered as a copyist on 19 March 1858, and she joined the ranks of women and men who set up their easels in the museum's galleries (Pl. 4). Morisot, like so many of her contemporaries, was attracted to the works of the Venetians and she copied Paolo Veronese's *Feast in the House of Simon* and *Calvary*.

The aspect of Guichard's instruction which had most appealed to the sisters was painting out of doors and they expressed an interest in developing this side of their work further. Guichard introduced them to the celebrated landscapist Camille Corot, who did not take formal pupils but delighted in having an audience of young painters to whom he imparted his ideas. One of the regular visitors to his studio was Camille Pissarro, to whom he had said: 'Above all one must study values ... for that is the basis of everything. ...' Values, here, are the tonal properties of colour on a scale from white to black. Corot had summed up his ideas about art in a letter of 1857: 'Beauty in art is truth steeped in the impression made upon us by the sight of nature. I am struck on seeing some place or other. While seeking conscious imitation I do not for an instant lose the emotion that first gripped me. Reality forms part of art, feeling completes it. ...'

7. Achille Oudinot. *Autumn in the Forest—Evening.* 1858. Oil on canvas, 70.4 × 108 cm. (27¾ × 42½ in.) Alençon, Musée des Beaux-Arts et de la Dentelle

Corot was at this time at the height of his fame. His approach to painting combined a Romantic belief in feeling and the imagination as the source of art with an insistence on close observation from nature. Women did not go to the regular informal gatherings in his studio as it would have been considered improper for them to do so, but, although he was usually notoriously unsociable, Corot became a regular visitor to the Morisot home, attending weekly dinners on Tuesdays at which he would advise the Morisot sisters about their work. The sisters established a warm relationship with their new teacher and managed to persuade their parents to spend the summer of 1861 at Ville d'Avray so that they could be near him. It was from Corot that they first became aware of the doctrine of naturalism which was to dominate so much of the art of the ensuing twenty years (Pl. 1). Corot, like many other teachers, gave his followers his own works to copy. These were usually not recent works, but paintings from twenty or even thirty years before. He set Berthe the task of copying his *View of Tivoli* of 1843 and expected the copy to be meticulously accurate (Pl. 5). Edma proved to be a more disciplined pupil than her sister and Corot made an exchange of pictures with her while insisting that Berthe redo a copy from which she had omitted one step of a staircase.

Sharing the ambition to become painters, the sisters were extremely close at this time. In the summer of 1862 they travelled together to the Pyrenees, and Yves and the rest of the family were aware of the special closeness which they enjoyed. Yves wrote to her sisters: 'Last night father said that we shall never be apprised of all the incidents of your trip, but that you will be telling them to each other for the next six months in the solitude and secrecy of your rooms. Anyone curious to know your impressions will have to listen at the keyhole.' In 1863 Edma did a portrait of Berthe working at her easel and she was later to become one of her sister's favourite models (Pl. 6).

Corot's influence on Morisot's works of the 1860s is evident. The subtle but clear palette, with its use of greens and greys and the mood of melancholy which such tonalities could evoke recall many of her teacher's works. In the summer of 1863, when Corot left Paris to paint in the countryside, he recommended that the sisters continue their instruction under Achilles François Oudinot, a landscapist whose work closely resembled Corot's own, as his image of a softly lit autumn evening, *Autumn in the Forest*, shows (Pl. 7). Oudinot was a close friend of the landscapist Daubigny, who lived and worked in the Auvers region. It was here that the Morisot sisters executed the first paintings which they were to submit to the Paris Salon. In the catalogue for the Salon of 1864, the sisters were listed as the pupils of Guichard and Oudinot. Edma's entries were *On the Banks of the Oise* and *Landscape: Effect of Evening*. Berthe's submissions were *A Souvenir of the Banks of the Oise* and *Old Path at Auvers* (Pl. 8). It was usual for aspiring young artists to seek to show their work at the Salon, the official forum for the exhibition of contemporary paintings in Paris. The Salons at this time were held in the vast Palais de l'Industrie. There were thirty rooms, crammed with paintings which hung from floor to ceiling. Huge crowds thronged to the exhibition—50,000 visitors on a Sunday afternoon were not uncommon and all the newspapers and periodicals devoted considerable space to Salon reviews. Most often, the work of newcomers, especially women, would pass unnoticed and Morisot must have been gratified to be given a mention in both *Le Courrier artistique* and *La Revue nationale et étrangère*. In the latter, Charles Asselineau remarked on the resemblance of her work to that of Corot.

In 1865 the sisters again showed at the Salon, Edma exhibiting *The Cliffs of Houlgate (Calvados)* and a flower still life and Berthe a still life and a study showing a young woman in a white dress at the edge of a stream. Mme Morisot described the vastness and anonymity of the exhibition halls in a letter to her eldest daughter:

> I had to go to a great deal of trouble to find Berthe and Edma's pictures.... Berthe's still life is all the less conspicuous because it is not hung in the hall with M's [works were generally hung alphabetically]. Edma's pot of flowers can barely be detected in one of the square rooms at the end, next to Guillemet's landscape. It cuts a sorry figure. . . . Berthe's Woman is well-

8. Berthe Morisot. *Old Path at Auvers*. 1863. Oil on canvas, 45 × 31 cm. (17¾ × 12¼ in.) Private collection

lighted, at least in the mornings, and does not look bad at all: I saw people pointing it out to one another. ... Edma's landscape has the honour of being on the line [hung at eye level].

Morisot received congratulations from the critic Gonzague Privat, and earned a backhanded compliment from another critic, Paul Mantz, who commented: 'Since it is not necessary to have had a long training in draughtsmanship in the academy in order to paint a copper pot, a candlestick, and a bunch of radishes, women succeed quite well in this type of domestic painting. Mlle Berthe Morisot brings to the task really a great deal of frankness with a delicate feeling for light and colours.' Mantz's prejudices on two fronts are revealed: not only his belief in the limitations of women's capacities but also his aversion to still life, still widely regarded as inferior to the more heroic Salon genres of history painting and the nude. If women were to be artists, it was thought that it was in the humble art of still life, especially flower painting, that they could succeed and many women did indeed excel in these genres.

In 1864 M. Morisot had been appointed chief councillor of the Cour des Comptes and the family moved house, although they remained in the Rue Franklin in Passy. The house stood in a beautiful garden in which M. Morisot had a studio built for his daughters. Such a gesture was a sure indication of the seriousness with which the sisters took their work. They devoted much of their time to painting, but for Edma this commitment to art was not to be a lifelong endeavour. After her marriage in 1869 to a naval officer, Adolphe Pontillon, she made the choice of relinquishing her activity as an artist for that of wife and mother. This choice was made with difficulty, and her letters to her sister express the sense of loss which she experienced: 'In my thoughts I follow you about in your studio, and wish that I could escape, were it only for a quarter of an hour, to breathe the air in which we lived for many long years.' Edma's decision was seen to be typical, while Berthe's continuing commitment to a life dedicated to art was regarded as unusual. When a friend of the family, Mme Chasseriau, sought to introduce Morisot and her mother to Charles Blanc, then director of the École des Beaux Arts, she found it necessary to point out that although the world in which the Morisots lived would have customarily distracted a young woman from serious pursuits, Berthe alone, unlike her two married sisters, had 'consecrated herself absolutely to painting'. In fact Morisot was one of many women to do this during her time. Unprecedented numbers of women became serious artists, although the social and critical context in which they worked continued both to obstruct their chances of success and to pressurize them to conform to the accepted norms of 'feminine' behaviour.

2 Morisot and her Circle

While copying at the Louvre Morisot came into contact with many of the artists with whom she was to develop lifelong associations. Among the painters to whom she was introduced in the late 1850s and 1860s were Carolus-Duran, who was already beginning to establish a reputation as a portraitist, Félix Bracquemond, and Henri Fantin-Latour. Bracquemond had been a pupil of Guichard and was to become one of the most prolific printmakers of his time, but in the 1860s he was still concentrating on painting. Fantin-Latour, a pupil of Lecoq de Boisbaudran, had been copying in the Louvre since 1852 and met the Morisot sisters in 1858. Through him, Morisot was introduced to Edouard Manet in the Louvre in 1867. Manet had already noticed Edma Morisot's work, and had heard gossip about the sisters. Mme Morisot wrote to Edma in 1867: 'Fantin expressed his admiration of your beauty, saying that he had never seen a creature as ravishing as you were a few years ago.... There was less talk about your painting, it seemed to me, than about your person. However, Manet mentioned the offer he had made to an art dealer when he saw something of yours that charmed him.'

Morisot already knew Manet's work: the notoriety which attached to him after his submission of *Olympia* to the Salon of 1865 ensured that she could hardly not have heard of him. Like Morisot, Manet came from an upper-middle-class background, and his father, a principal private secretary to the minister of justice, occupied a position similar to that of M. Morisot. This meant that, despite the scandal which surrounded his professional life, Mme Morisot would have regarded him and his family as suitable socially. The Morisots, mother and two daughters, soon became part of the Manets' circle, attending the gatherings arranged by Manet's mother, and Mme Morisot and Mme Manet became friends.

Manet often used his friends and family as models for his paintings, and in 1869 asked Morisot to pose for *The Balcony* (Pl. 9), shown at the Salon of that

9. Edouard Manet. *The Balcony*. 1869. Oil on canvas, 169 × 125 cm. (66½ × 49¼ in.) Paris, Musée d'Orsay

10. Edouard Manet. *Portrait of Berthe Morisot*. Related to portrait of 1872. Lithograph, printed 1884, 21.8 × 16.4 cm. (8½ × 6½ in.) Paris, Bibliothèque Nationale

11. Pierre Auguste Renoir. *Berthe Morisot and her Daughter*. 1894. Crayon on paper. Paris, Musée du Petit Palais

12. Edouard Manet. *Eva Gonzalès*. 1870. Oil on canvas, 191 × 133 cm. (75¼ × 52⅜ in.) London, National Gallery

13. Berthe Morisot. *Portrait of Edma*. 1870. Oil on canvas, 56 × 46 cm. (22 × 18¼ in.) London, Courtauld Institute Galleries (Princes Gate Collection)

14. Berthe Morisot. *The Artist's Sister at a Window*. 1869. Oil on canvas, 55 × 46 cm. (21½ × 18 in.) Washington D.C., National Gallery of Art, Ailsa Mellon Bruce Collection

year. This was the first of several occasions on which she acted as his model. *Le Repos*, shown at the Salon of 1873, was another of his Salon paintings for which she modelled. In *The Balcony*, the standing female figure was modelled by the nineteen-year-old violinist Fanny Claus, also a member of the Manet circle, while the painter Antoine Guillemet posed for the male figure. Like Morisot, Fanny Claus had rejected the prevalent idea that while art and music were accomplishments befitting young middle-class women, they were not to be pursued professionally. Morisot, Claus, and Guillemet found posing for Manet an arduous task. He required so many sittings that finally, as Mme Morisot told Edma, both Guillemet and Claus assured him: 'It's perfect—there is nothing more to be done over.'

Morisot's striking appearance, with her dark eyes and hair, was commented on by numerous writers and critics, and even in the latter part of her life, she was often described by comparison with her image in Manet's portraits (Pl. 10). The Symbolist critic Henri de Régnier, for instance, remembering his visits to Morisot in the 1890s, wrote: 'Tall and slender, of great distinction of manner, an artist of delicate and subtle talent, Berthe Morisot was not, when I knew her, the strange creature with dark hair whose features Manet had captured in his famous painting *Le Balcon*. Her hair had whitened, but her face had kept its enigmatic singularity and its fine regularity, her taciturn melancholy expression and its constrained wildness.' It was the directness of the gaze and the sultriness of expression, so at odds with the conventional image of a young middle-class woman, which led Morisot herself to write of Manet's painting of her: 'I am more strange than ugly. It seems that the epithet of *femme fatale* has been circulating among the curious....'

Manet never painted Morisot at work, and in none of the various images of her by other members of her circle is she shown at work (Pl. 11). Her friends considered it inappropriate to depict her as a professional artist, preferring to represent her in a manner in keeping with the conventions governing the behaviour of middle-class women. When Manet painted his pupil Eva Gonzalès seated at an easel, brushes and mahlstick in hand (Pl. 12), he chose to show her fashionably attired in a white dress which belies the idea that she is working.

Morisot herself did not paint portraits of her male colleagues, since it was thought inappropriate for an unmarried woman to ask a man to sit for her. Her sister Edma was her favourite model in the late 1860s and early 1870s (Pl. 13). Morisot depicted her in works in various media. During Edma's confinement, which necessitated long passive days in the family home, Morisot made some of her most searching portraits of her, including *The Artist's Sister at a Window* of 1869 (Pl. 14). After the birth of Edma's daughter Jeanne, Morisot made several watercolours of her sister with her child, among them *Woman and Child Seated in a Field* (Pl. 15), which was shown at the first Impressionist exhibition, and *The Artist's Sister Edma with her Daughter Jeanne* (Pl. 16), as well as a pastel portrait of Edma alone, during her second confinement, *Portrait of Mme Pontillon* (Pl. 17). Her sister Yves and her children were also favoured models, although they were less frequently in Paris. *On the Balcony* (Pl. 18) represents

Edma with Yves's daughter Paule looking out over the Champ de Mars from the Morisot family home in the Rue Franklin.

Morisot was not included either in Fantin-Latour's celebration of the Batignolles group, *The Batignolles Studio* (Pl. 19), painted in 1870, or in Frédéric Bazille's *The Artist's Studio, Rue de la Condamine* of the same date. Both these paintings show Manet, Bazille, Monet, Renoir, Edmond Maître, and the novelist Émile Zola. Through her friendship with Manet and with Fantin-Latour, Morisot knew most if not all these men by this date, but she could not participate in the easy interchange of ideas in which male artists engaged in the cafés or in their studios. Her class and gender would have made her presence in such places improper. Her more formal, chaperoned meetings with the two members of the Batignolles circle who were of a similar class to her own, Manet and Degas, were crucial to the development of her artistic ideas in the late 1860s, for it was only at such meetings that she could participate in the artistic debates of the day.

The regular salons held in *haut bourgeois* circles served as a bridge between two worlds generally conceived of at this date as being entirely separate, the 'woman's' world of the home and the 'man's' world of business and commerce. At these gatherings, women would usually have been expected to be decorative and charming, but a part of the function of the salons was to cultivate the art of conversation, and Morisot must have tested her own strongly held beliefs about clear, high-toned painting, often the result of outdoor studies, in discussions with painters and sculptors at her own parents' salons, and at her regular attendances both at Mme Manet's Thursday salons, and at the Belgian painter Alfred Stevens's Wednesday parties. Both Manet and Degas were frequent visitors at her parents' home. Degas painted a portrait of her sister, Yves Gobillard Morisot (Pl. 20). Mme Morisot's social gatherings were a meeting place for people such as Jules Ferry, then a journalist, later prime minister of France; Dr. Émile Blanche, whose clinic for mental patients was near the Morisots' Passy home; the composer Emmanuel Chabrier; the painter Léon Riesener and his daughters Rosalie and Louise, whom Morisot painted; the sculptors Aimé Millet and Marcello, Duchess of Colonna, both of whom gave Morisot instruction in sculpture; and Pierre Puvis de Chavannes, whose large-scale mural paintings were to make him renowned during the Third Republic. Puvis de Chavannes and Morisot did not share artistic beliefs, but she admired his paintings nonetheless, telling Edma: 'I am the only one at our house who likes Puvis's paintings. They are thought to be uninteresting, cold.' He was devoted to her, and corresponded regularly with her both before and after her marriage.

It is often held that Morisot was Manet's pupil, but while she admired his work, there is nothing to suggest that this was so. Manet was an important influence on many of the younger painters of his day. In him they saw an artist who had invested contemporary life with the seriousness normally accorded to historical, mythological, or religious subjects, and who had challenged the academic preference for highly finished, subtly modulated surfaces with his painterly, dramatically lit arrangements. Morisot, like Monet, Renoir, and

15. Berthe Morisot. *Woman and Child Seated in a Field*. 1871. Watercolour on paper, 19.5 × 24 cm. (7⅝ × 9½ in.) Private collection

16. Berthe Morisot. *The Artist's Sister Edma with her Daughter Jeanne.* 1872. Watercolour on paper, 25 × 26 cm. (9⅞ × 10¼ in.) Washington D.C., National Gallery of Art, Ailsa Mellon Bruce Collection

Sisley, respected Manet's achievements and would have welcomed his advice and interest, but she, like them, was not his formal pupil. In 1870 she asked his opinion of a painting she intended to submit to the Salon jury, *The Mother and Sister of the Artist* (Pl. 21), and he offered to look at it and advise her. The painting represents her mother and her sister Edma, who, after her marriage to Adolphe Pontillon early in 1869, had, according to the prevailing custom, returned to her parental home to await the birth of her first child. Morisot had been feeling insecure about this painting—she described herself as 'tired, weary'—and she had already asked Pierre Puvis de Chavannes to comment on the work. He had recommended that she 'put some accents on the mother's head', and had complimented her on the remainder of the painting. Manet, however, did not restrict himself to advice. He set about retouching the painting, and Morisot's fury when recounting this incident to her sister indicates that she neither regarded herself as his pupil, nor welcomed his intervention: 'He cracked a thousand jokes, laughed like a madman, handed me the palette, took it back; finally by five o'clock in the afternoon we had made the prettiest caricature that was ever seen.... And now I am left confounded. My only hope is that I shall be rejected. Mother thinks this episode funny, but I find it agonizing.' However, the picture was in fact accepted by the jury, and by 1874 Morisot had reassessed the extent of Manet's changes and felt able to submit the painting to the first Impressionist exhibition.

When Manet admired her other submission to the Salon of 1870, *The Harbour at Lorient* (Pl. 22), painted during the summer of 1869, with Edma serving as the model, she made him a gift of it, and he was later to loan it to the first Impressionist exhibition. Painted at least in part in the open air, it may have helped to awaken Manet's own interest in *plein-airism*. At this date, Morisot's concern with recording fleeting atmospheric effects out of doors and applying the lessons of *plein-air* study in paintings, rather than small watercolour studies or sketches, was more developed than Manet's own.

As is discussed in chapter three, Morisot was a founder member of the group which organized the independent group show held in 1874; this became known as the first Impressionist exhibition. Her close professional association with her Impressionist colleagues continued throughout the 1870s, and she was an integral part of the Impressionist group, present at the meetings held to arrange the exhibitions and to discuss questions of policy. In 1877, for instance, Degas wrote to her: 'The meeting is at five o'clock. A momentous question is to be discussed: is it permitted to exhibit at the Salon as well as with us? Very important!' However, she was of course excluded from more informal studio discussions, as well as from the lively and sometimes turbulent debates which now raged at the Café de la Nouvelle-Athenès. Manet and Degas, still her closest friends and habitués at the cafe, may have related some of the talk to her. In December 1874 she married Eugène Manet, Edouard's brother, and the ties of friendship were even further strengthened by a family bond. Manet's small painting, *The Bunch of Violets* (Pl. 23), is a testament to their friendship and mutual regard.

In the late 1870s, Morisot developed a friendship with her Impressionist colleague, the American painter Mary Cassatt. Cassatt had bought one of her paintings in 1878, and first exhibited with the Impressionists in 1879, the only occasion on which Morisot did not participate, following the birth of her daughter Julie on 14 November 1878. In the autumn of 1879 Cassatt wrote to her: 'I am so happy that you have done so much work, you will reclaim your place at the exposition with *éclat*, I am very envious of your talent I assure you.' In 1882 Eugène Manet wrote to Morisot: 'Yesterday I met Miss Cassatt at the exhibition [the seventh Impressionist exhibition]. She seems to wish to be more intimate with us. She asks to do portraits of Bibi [Julie] and of you. I said, yes, gladly, on conditions of reciprocity.' This project does not appear to have been realized. The two women were particularly close in 1889 and 1890, when both were absorbed with the problems of making colour prints. There is now no trace of any colour prints by Morisot, but she made a number of drypoints in these years, including *The Duck* (Pl. 24). In April 1890 Cassatt urged Morisot to see the exhibition of Japanese prints at the École des Beaux Arts: 'Seriously, you must not miss that. You who want to make color prints you couldn't dream of anything more beautiful.' She added as a postscript: 'You *must* see the Japanese—*come as soon as you can.*' Cassatt's informal tone indicates an ease and affection between herself and Morisot by this date.

Morisot and Renoir had been on cordial terms during the 1870s, but during the 1880s a close friendship developed. Renoir separated his private from his artistic life to the extent that he concealed the existence of Aline Charigot and their son Pierre, born in 1885, from Morisot until 1891, by which date he had married Aline. Morisot had commented in a notebook in January 1886 on a series of Renoir's drawings of a mother and child without any indication that she was aware of the identity of the models. On one of his frequent visits to Mézy, where the Morisot-Manets had rented a house, Renoir was accompanied by Aline and Pierre, whom he failed to introduce formally, causing Morisot some consternation. In 1887 Renoir was commissioned by Morisot and Eugène Manet to paint a portrait of Julie, for which several preparatory drawings exist. The painting, as Julie Manet recalled many years later, was painted 'bit by bit, one day my head and a little of the background, another day my dress and cat'. Morisot herself executed both a pastel and a drypoint after Renoir's portrait in 1889 (Pl. 25). Their friendship was so close that Morisot named Renoir as one of Julie's guardians in the will she made after the death of her husband in 1892. The poet Stéphane Mallarmé was named as the other.

Mallarmé had been one of Edouard Manet's closest friends, and after the painter's death in 1883, he became an intimate friend both of Morisot and of Eugène Manet, visiting them regularly at their home on the Rue de Villejust. He admired Morisot's work, and was instrumental in persuading the state to purchase *Young Woman Dressed for the Ball* (Pl. 26) at the sale of part of Théodore Duret's collection in 1894. This was the first of Morisot's paintings to enter a French national collection. Morisot discussed the possibility of illustrating one of Mallarmé's prose poems, *Le Nenuphar blanc*, for an edition involving

17. Berthe Morisot. *Portrait of Mme Pontillon*. 1871. Pastel on paper, 81 × 65 cm. (31⅞ × 25⅝ in.) Paris, Musée du Louvre, Cabinet des Dessins

18. Berthe Morisot. *On the Balcony*. 1872. Watercolour over graphite on paper, 20.6 × 17.5 cm. (8⅛ × 6⅞ in.) Chicago, The Art Institute, gift in memory of Charles Netcher II, 1933

the collaboration of several painters, including Renoir. She found his writing difficult to understand and wrote: 'It would be kind of you to come to dinner on Thursday. Renoir and I are quite bewildered; we need explanations for the illustrations.' Mallarmé replied: 'I am disturbed by your bewilderment: fortunately, your smile appears in the background...'. The project did not materialize, but Morisot executed a number of drypoints with Mallarmé's poems in mind (Pl. 28).

Mallarmé's letter to Morisot reveals that her physical appearance was rarely forgotten, and that the obligation to compliment and flatter her as a woman was almost always present. A rare exception to this was Degas (referred to as 'Monsieur Degas' in her correspondence even when he was a regular visitor to her home), who defied conventional codes of behaviour. On one occasion in her youth, as Morisot had recounted to Edma: 'He came over and sat beside me, pretending that he was going to court me. But the courting was confined to a

19. Henri Fantin-Latour. *The Batignolles Studio.* 1870. Oil on canvas, 204 × 273 cm. (80⅜ × 107⅝ in.) Paris, Musée d'Orsay

20. Edgar Degas. *Yves Gobillard Morisot*. 1869. Oil on canvas, 53 × 64 cm. (20⅞ × 25¼ in.) New York, Metropolitan Museum of Art, Bequest of Mrs H. O. Havemeyer, 1929. The H. O. Havemeyer Collection

long commentary on Solomon's proverb "Woman is the desolation of the righteous".'

As her mother had done in the 1860s, Morisot herself in the last decade of her life held regular soirées. Every Thursday an intellectual and artistic circle gathered, first at the Rue de Villejust, and after Eugène's death in 1892, at Morisot's new home on the Rue Wéber; members included Mallarmé; Villiers de l'Isle-Adam before his death in 1889; some of the younger Parnassian poets and writers such as Teodor de Wyzewa and Henri de Régnier; Monet, on his visits to Paris from Giverny; Degas; occasionally Whistler; and Renoir. Other guests included Émile Ollivier, the politician, a friend of Eugène and Edouard

21. Berthe Morisot. *The Mother and Sister of the Artist*. 1869–70. Oil on canvas, 101 × 81.8 cm. (39¾ × 32¼ in.) Washington D.C., National Gallery of Art, Chester Dale Collection

22. Berthe Morisot. *The Harbour at Lorient*. 1869. Oil on canvas, 43.5 × 73 cm. (17⅛ × 28¾ in.) Washington D.C., National Gallery of Art, Ailsa Mellon Bruce Collection

Manet since the 1850s, when he had travelled to Italy with them; Jules de Jouy, a magistrate who was a cousin of Manet's; Morisot's friend of long standing, Mme Hubard (Pl. 27); and the painter and collector Henri Lerolle with his daughters Yvonne and Christine. It was in Morisot's studio at the Rue de Villejust that Mallarmé read his celebrated lecture on Villiers de l'Isle-Adam in 1890, the year after the poet's death, a lecture so obscure that Degas commented angrily that he had understood nothing of it. At these gatherings Morisot, as the hostess, was conspicuous for her silence. Accounts by de Régnier and by Paul Valéry, who married her niece Jeanne after Morisot's death, construct her as a muse, and as a sphinx-like figure, an 'intent and reserved personality whose grace and remoteness combined to create extraordinary charm'. During a decade when many other women, even those of her class, were loosening the strictures that had

23. Edouard Manet. *The Bunch of Violets*. 1872. Oil on canvas, 22 × 27 cm. (8⅝ × 10⅝ in.) Paris, Private collection

24. Berthe Morisot. *The Duck.*
1888. Drypoint. 13.7 × 10 cm. (5⅜
× 4 in.) London, British Museum,
Department of Prints and
Drawings

25. Berthe Morisot. *Girl with Cat.*
1889. Drypoint, 14.5 × 11.3 cm.
(5¾ × 4½ in.) London, British
Museum, Department of Prints
and Drawings

26. Berthe Morisot. *Young Woman Dressed for the Ball.* 1879. Oil on canvas, 71 × 54 cm. (28 × 21¼ in.) Paris, Musée d'Orsay

27. Berthe Morisot. *Portrait of Mme Hubard.* 1874. Oil on canvas, 50.5 × 81 cm. (19$\frac{7}{8}$ × 31$\frac{7}{8}$ in.) Copenhagen, Ordrupgaardsamlingen

28. Berthe Morisot. *The Lake at the Bois de Boulogne*. 1888. Drypoint. 15.5 × 11.5 cm. (6⅛ × 4⅝ in.) London, British Museum, Department of Prints and Drawings

bound them, Morisot retained the conventionality and correctness of behaviour of her youth. She joked with Mallarmé that one day 'Julie and I will dress as men and attend one of your Tuesdays [Mallarmé's literary evenings]', but in the event, she did not feel able to attend a male gathering. 'No, decidedly, the schoolbench would intimidate us too much,' she declared.

The reaction of her close circle to her death on 2 March 1895 testifies to the high regard in which they held her. Renoir learned of her death, as Julie Manet recalled many years later, when he was 'in the midst of painting alongside Cézanne . . . he closed his paintbox and took the train—I have never forgotten the way he came into my room on the Rue Wéber and took me in his arms...'. Mallarmé sent telegrams to Octave Mirbeau, Henri de Régnier, Degas, and others: 'I am the bearer of very sad news. Our poor friend, Mme Eugène Manet, Berthe Morisot is dead...'. Pissarro wrote to his son Lucien: 'Still in Paris, because I want to attend the funeral of our old comrade Berthe Morisot.... You can hardly conceive how surprised we all were and how moved, too, by the disappearance of this distinguished woman, who had such a splendid feminine talent and who brought honour to our impressionist group which is vanishing—like all things. Poor Mme Morisot, the public hardly knows her!'

3 Morisot and Impressionism

Morisot's studies with Corot and Oudinot had led her to conclude that her main interest was in painting out of doors (*en plein air*). In this, she was following what was already an established tradition, furthered by Corot, of recording effects of nature either for reference purposes or as preparations for paintings done in the studio. Corot's teacher, Achille-Etna Michallon, was himself a pupil of Pierre-Henri de Valenciennes, who had revived the genre of historical landscape painting. Valenciennes had begun to develop painterly means of recording effects of changing light, and in his *Elémens de perspective pratique* [*Elements of Practical Perspective*], first published in 1799–1800 (revised in 1820), he had outlined his ideas about aerial perspective and the importance of the outdoor oil sketch. This treatise was widely read during the nineteenth century, and either Corot or Oudinot may well have recommended it to the Morisot sisters. Much later, in 1883, Camille Pissarro sent a copy of it to his son Lucien, describing it as 'still the best and most practical' account of the principles of perspective. Corot's practice was along the lines suggested by Valenciennes. By the 1860s his maxim, 'Never lose the first impression which has moved you' was standard advice. Thomas Couture, Manet's teacher from 1850 to 1856, urged his pupils to work rapidly and to 'keep the first vivid impression', while Horace Lecoq de Boisbaudran, Fantin-Latour's teacher, recognized that it was impossible to convey immediacy without training the memory. He developed a system to train this faculty, believing that 'Without it, innumerable subjects are entirely beyond us. How else can animals, clouds, water, rapid movement, expression, or passing effects of colour be recorded?'

Morisot's preference for working outdoors and trying to convey a sense of immediacy, therefore, was not in itself novel. Working out of doors in the country permitted her a freedom impossible in the city, where she had constantly to be chaperoned. The family's summer visits to the newly developed bathing resorts in Normandy gave her opportunities to sketch and paint without hindrance. On a visit to Beuzeval in 1864, for instance, her brother Tiburce

29. Berthe Morisot. *The Seine below the Pont d'Iéna*. 1866. Oil on canvas, 50.8 × 80 cm. (20 × 31½ in.) Montgomery, Alabama, Collection of Mr Adolph Weil, Jr.

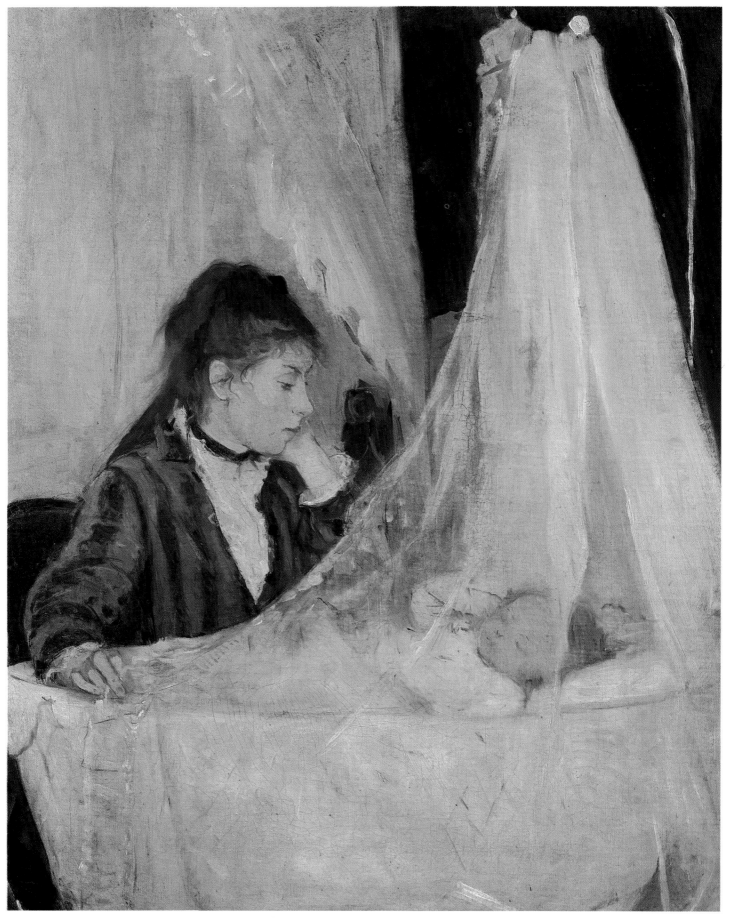

30. Berthe Morisot. *The Cradle*. 1872. Oil on canvas, 56 × 46 cm. (22 × 18⅛ in.) Paris, Musée d'Orsay

31. Camille Corot. *L'Eglise de Marissel.* 1867. Oil on canvas, 55 × 42 cm. (22 × 16¾ in.) Paris, Musée du Louvre

recalled: 'She would vanish for entire days among the cliffs, pursuing one motif after another, according to the hour and the slant of the sun.' As her Salon submissions of the 1860s, for example, *The Seine below the Pont d'Iéna* (Pl. 29), shown in 1867, indicate, she did not separate these outdoor studies rigidly from more formal studio paintings. This was in part because of the restrictions placed on her art education by her gender, which meant that she did not attempt those genres regarded as the most challenging. In part, too, by the late 1860s the rigid categorizations of Salon paintings were gradually changing, and a changing emphasis in teaching was beginning to be reflected in the appearance of paintings which shared Morisot's own concern with apparent spontaneity and direct observation. Corot's *L'Eglise de Marissel* (Pl. 31), for instance, shown at the same Salon as Morisot's painting, is less formal and less obviously part of the

32. Paul Cézanne. *A Modern Olympia*. 1873. Oil on canvas, 46 × 55 cm. (18⅛ × 21⅝ in.) Paris, Musée d'Orsay

tradition of historical landscape painting than many of his earlier Salon entries had been.

With this gradual shift came confusion. As the massive scale of rejections which occasioned the Salon des Refusés in 1863 had shown, selection or rejection by Salon juries often seemed arbitrary, and Monet, Renoir, and Pissarro all suffered rejections during this decade. It was because they could not be sure that their work would ever be on view at the Salon, much less that it would be noticed by the critics and the public, that 'a group of young people', as Frédéric Bazille described them to his parents, began in 1867 to plan exhibitions independent of the Salon and its jury system. Morisot may already have been a part of this group, although it is more likely that her involvement dates from later on: Bazille commented that the group consisted of a 'dozen talented people'. Morisot's record of acceptance at the Salon and the fact that she did not depend

33. Berthe Morisot. *Hide-and-Seek*. 1873. Oil on canvas, 45 × 55 cm. (17¾ × 21⅝ in.) New York, Collection of Mrs John Hay Whitney

34. Berthe Morisot. *On the Lawn*. 1874. Pastel on paper, 73 × 92 cm. (28¾ × 36¼ in.) Paris, Musée du Petit Palais

on sales for her livelihood meant that finding an alternative method of exhibition was not a question of survival. It was her belief in the importance of observation and of *peinture claire*, the expressing of light by a predominantly luminous, blond tonality, very different from the chiaroscuro of so many Salon paintings, that made Morisot cast in her lot with this group of artists, and by the time the group was formally constituted, on 27 December 1873, she was one of the core members. Her commitment, both to the new form of exhibition and to an approach to painting which she had already been pursuing prior to meeting her colleagues, was unswerving. She did not heed Manet's or Fantin-Latour's opposition to the new group's exhibition plans, nor their urging that she reconsider her decision to show with them, and she was unmoved by the views of two of her former teachers regarding this affiliation. Guichard advised her to dissociate herself from 'the so-called school of the future', while Corot told Antoine Guillemet: 'You have done very well to escape from that gang.'

The first exhibition of the *Société anonyme des artistes peintres, sculpteurs, graveurs, etc.* opened in the premises formerly occupied by the photographer Nadar on the Boulevard des Capucines on 15 April 1874. Two days later, Émile d'Hervilly wrote in the radical newspaper *Le Rappel* that the administration and the Salon jury were 'the two cripplers of French art', and contrasted the work on view at the Boulevard des Capucines to 'the nauseating banalities of the academic routine', concluding: 'One cannot encourage this daring undertaking too much.' Edouard Drumont, writing in *Le Petit Journal*, agreed: 'What pleases us is the initiative taken by these artists who, without recriminations, protests, or polemics, opened a room and said to the crowds, "We see like this, we understand art this way, come in, look, and buy if you like".' Morisot was represented at this exhibition, now known, of course, as the first Impressionist exhibition, by nine works. They were oils, watercolours, and pastels, and included the two paintings previously shown at the 1870 Salon, *The Harbour at Lorient* (Pl. 22) and *The Mother and Sister of the Artist* (Pl. 21). The other oils were *The Cradle* (Pl. 30) and *Hide-and-Seek* (Pl. 33). Morisot used the opportunity afforded by a juryless exhibition to show a range of her work: landscape, portraiture, and figure paintings; work of recent origin and work executed before the Franco-Prussian War. The rigidity of the Salon system would have made such a diverse and extensive showing impossible, and over the next twelve years, one of the reasons for the continuing existence of the independent group exhibitions was the potential they offered participants to display a variety of work, a potential which Morisot, no less than her male colleagues, exploited from the first.

The diversity of work on view at the first exhibition was heightened by the manner of the display. The spaciousness of the hanging, in contrast to the dense crowding of the Salon's walls, emphasized the contrasts between works. Morisot's *The Cradle* hung next to Paul Cézanne's *A Modern Olympia* (Pl. 32), a work identical in size, and the contrast between Morisot's evocation of maternity and Cézanne's erotic fantasy so startled Guichard that he wrote to Morisot's mother: 'If Mlle Berthe must do something violent, she should, rather than burn everything she has done so far, pour some petrol on the new tendencies. How could she exhibit a work of art as exquisitely delicate as hers side by side with *Le Rêve du célibataire* [*A Modern Olympia*]? ... to negate all the efforts, all the aspirations, all the past dreams that have filled one's life, is madness. Worse, it is almost a sacrilege.'

Morisot was not deterred either by Guichard's remarks or by other critical comments, and on 24 March 1875 she made a public declaration of her belief in and adherence to Impressionism when she participated in an auction sale at the Hôtel Drouot. The public's outrage at the work was extreme, and the prices all the works achieved were low. Morisot fared somewhat better than Renoir, Monet, or Sisley, and her *Interior* fetched 480 francs, the highest price of the sale. It was purchased by Ernest Hoschedé, an entrepreneur who was one of the first to amass a collection of Impressionist paintings. Other buyers included Morisot's brother-in-law, Gustave Manet, who bought a pastel, *On the Lawn* (Pl. 34) and a view of Petites Dalles; Henri Rouart, the painter and engineer, who bought *In a Villa at the Seaside* (Pl. 35); and the naturalist painter Ernest Duez, who bought *Chasing Butterflies* (Pl. 36).

With the decision to hold a second exhibition in 1876, Morisot and her colleagues declared themselves a group with recognizable and collective aims and practices. The first exhibition had been an attempt to gain visibility, perhaps still with the idea of re-entering the forum of the Salon, but by 1876 the critics' insistence on the lack of finish of the works, combined with the political implications of the name 'Intransigents', used as frequently as the term 'Impressionist', meant that independent exhibitions appeared to be the only avenue open to the artists which would ensure that their work could be seen. The exhibition was on show at the premises of the dealer Paul Durand-Ruel at 11 Rue Le Peletier during April. As before, it had a neutral title, 'The second exhibition of paintings by MM. ...', but once again, the terms 'Impressionist' and 'Intransigent' were used in the press.

Morisot's commitment to remaining outside the Salon system is indicated by the size and range of her submission. She showed seventeen works, more than any of her colleagues except Degas, who was represented by twenty-four works, including a sketch for his portrait of Yves Gobillard Morisot (Pl. 20), and a portrait of Eugène Manet, and Monet, who had eighteen works on view. Her entries appear to have been divided among two of the three exhibition rooms, with the watercolours and pastels in the first room, and the oil paintings in the second. The works included landscapes and figure paintings, among them *At the Ball* (Pl. 37) and *Hanging the Laundry out to Dry* (Pl. 38).

The third exhibition, held in 1877 in a five-room apartment rented by Gustave Caillebotte at 6 Rue Le Peletier, was the first to be designated an 'Impressionist' exhibition. Morisot's works shared the third of these rooms with Pissarro's *The Côte des Boeufs at L'Hermitage, near Pontoise* (Pl. 39); Renoir's *Ball at the Moulin de la Galette*; and sixteen works by Cézanne, including *Head of a Man; Study* (Pl. 40), a portrait of the collector Victor Chocquet. Morisot showed several figure paintings, including *Head of a Girl*, now known as *Woman with Fan* (Pl. 41); *Psyche* (Pl. 42); and *Lady at her Toilet* (Pl. 47). The contrast

35. Berthe Morisot. *In a Villa at the Seaside.* 1874. Oil on canvas, 51 × 61 cm. (20⅛ × 24 in.) Pasadena, Museum of Art, Norton Simon Art Foundation

36. Berthe Morisot. *Chasing Butterflies*. 1874. Oil on canvas, 47 × 56 cm. (18½ × 22 in.) Paris, Musée d'Orsay

between her paintings, and not only Cézanne's paintings, but also the densely worked, multi-layered surface of the Pissarro landscape was extreme, and serves as a reminder of the range of work which could be encompassed within the label of 'Impressionism'. The differences were also an indication of the divisions between the various members of the group, which began to surface with the organization of a fourth show, planned for 1878, to coincide with the Universal Exhibition of that year, but which finally opened on 10 April 1879.

This was the only Impressionist exhibition in which Morisot did not participate. She had been undecided about whether or not to show until shortly before the opening, when her name still appeared on a list of exhibitors sent by the Italian critic Diego Martelli to a friend in Florence. Early in April Degas wrote to Félix Bracquemond: 'There is one room with *fans*, do you understand Mme Bracquemond [the painter Marie Bracquemond]? Up to now, Pissarro, Mlle Morisot, and I are depositing things there. You and your wife should contribute too.' Morisot's absence may have been due to illness. After the birth of Julie in November of the previous year, she was often depressed. As she wrote to her sister Yves: '. . . my life is becoming complicated, I have little time, and then I have days of melancholy, my black days when I am afraid to take up my pen for fear of being dull.'

She returned to the independent exhibitions in 1880, with a submission of paintings, watercolours, and a fan, which was favourably received. Among her submission was a pair, evocatively entitled *Summer* and *Winter* (Pls. 43, 44), which suggest that she was departing from the emphasis on the immediate and the specific which had characterized her work of the earlier 1870s. While obviously contemporary in subject matter, the titles evoke the generic and symbolic. Alfred Stevens's contemporary *Seasons* (Pl. 45), and Manet's later *Spring* and *Autumn* (Pl. 46), similarly, are titled in this way in order to transform the figure into allegory.

The sixth exhibition in 1881 was held in a series of cramped rooms at 35 Boulevard des Capucines. Although the address was the same as that of the first exhibition, the accommodation, in an annexe, was markedly different, and so too was the composition of the group. Monet did not participate, Renoir and Sisley had chosen to show at the Salon, and Caillebotte had withdrawn after disputes with Degas about the participation of Jean-François Raffaëlli. Morisot's submission of seven works probably included *The Wet Nurse Angèle Feeding Julie Manet* (Pl. 48), a landscape, and two pastel sketches. Her name was often linked in critical accounts with that of Mary Cassatt, a relatively recent recruit to the independents' ranks. The two women were seen as a pair, and Elie de Mont, writing for *La Civilisation*, went so far as to claim that they were the only two interesting artists exhibiting. Morisot's position within the Impressionist ranks was also recognized by Gustave Geffroy, who declared: 'No one represents Impressionism with more refined talent or with more authority than Morisot.'

Paul Durand-Ruel undertook the organization of the seventh exhibition himself. It was held at the Salons du Panorama de Reichshoffen on the Rue Saint-Honoré. The show was, as Pissarro noted, 'a necessity' both for the dealer and for the artists, not only financially but also to secure their reputations as painters. The economic slump in France precipitated by the failure of the Union-Générale bank earlier in the year had badly affected sales, and the artists who participated acknowledged that they had to present their best work or face the failure of their enterprise. As Monet wrote to Durand-Ruel: 'At the point where we are now an exhibition must be extremely well done or not take place at all....' Morisot, who was in Nice when the final arrangements and hanging took place, entrusted the organization of her submission to her husband. Shortly after the opening, he wrote: 'Duret, who knows what he is talking about, thinks that this year's exhibition is the best your group has ever had. This is also my opinion.' Although only nine works by Morisot were listed in the catalogue, there were twelve on view. The identification of these paintings is uncertain, but one of them may have been *Peasant Hanging the Washing* (Pl. 51).

The eighth and final exhibition of the independents, held in 1886, marked the swansong of Impressionism as a group movement. The original group had over the twelve years since the first show redefined their position as painters in a variety of ways. Monet and Renoir were by now exhibiting with the dealer Georges Petit, attempting to free themselves from total dependence on Durand-Ruel, and did not participate in the eighth exhibition, while Pissarro had aligned himself with Seurat and Signac, and described his former colleagues as 'romantic Impressionists'. Morisot sent a varied selection of work, including oils, water-colours, drawings, and fans, to this exhibition. Among them was *In the Dining Room* (Pl. 52). She had now come to represent, as the critic Félix Fénéon declared, 'impressionism as it was shown in previous manifestations'.

Some critics in 1886 discerned in her work evidence of concerns which in the next decade would be labelled 'symbolist'. Jean Ajalbert, the poet and critic, noted: '... she eliminates cumbersome epithets and heavy adverbs in her terse sentence. Everything is subject and verb. She has a kind of telegraphic style ...', while to Octave Mirbeau, her work provided '... a few scanty traces to create complete, disquieting evocations'. Over the years of the independent exhibitions, however, Morisot's approach to painting had been remarkably consistent. The sketchiness of handling in her work was remarked on frequently, both by favourable and by hostile critics, and the comments made by Jules Castagnary and by Louis Leroy at the first exhibition are noteworthy not only for their similarity but for their prefiguring of a refrain. Castagnary commented: 'Berthe Morisot has wit to the tips of her fingers, especially at her fingertips. What fine artistic feeling! You cannot find more graceful images handled more deliberately and delicately than *The Cradle* and *Hide-and-Seek*. I would add that here the execution is in complete accord with the idea to be expressed.' Leroy declared: 'Now take Mlle Morisot! That young lady is not interested in reproducing trifling details. When she has a hand to paint, she makes exactly as many brushstrokes lengthwise as there are fingers, and the business is done.'

Two years later, Alfred de Lostalot wrote: 'Given her delicate colour and the adroitly daring play of her brush with light, it is a real pity to see this artist give up her work when it is only barely sketched because she is so easily satisfied with

37. Berthe Morisot. *At the Ball.* 1875. Oil on canvas, 62 × 52 cm. (24⅜ × 20½ in.) Paris, Musée Marmottan

38. Berthe Morisot. *Hanging the Laundry out to Dry*. 1875. Oil on canvas, 33 × 40.6 cm. (13 × 16 in.) Washington D.C., National Gallery of Art, Collection of Mr and Mrs Paul Mellon

39. Camille Pissarro. *The Côte des Boeufs at L'Hermitage, near Pontoise*. 1877. Oil on canvas, 115 × 87.5 cm. (45¼ × 34½ in.)
London, National Gallery

40. Paul Cézanne. *Head of a Man; Study.* 1876–77. Oil on canvas, 45.7 × 36.8 cm. (18 × 14½ in.) New York, Private collection

41. Berthe Morisot. *Woman with Fan (Head of a Girl).* 1876. Oil on canvas, 62 × 52 cm. (24⅜ × 20½ in.) Collection of Mr and Mrs Alexander Lewyt

42. Berthe Morisot. *Psyche*. 1876. Oil on canvas, 64 × 54 cm. (25¼ × 21¼ in.) Lugano, Thyssen-Bornemisza Collection, Switzerland

it.' In commenting on what they saw as the lack of finish of her work, the critics sought to find an answer not in the debate about what constituted a sketch (*esquisse*) or a painting (*tableau*)—a matter of some moment not only for Morisot but also for her colleagues, especially Monet—but in her femininity. Paul de Charry complimented Morisot on her skill in a review in 1880, and then posed the question: 'With this talent, why does she not take the trouble to finish?' His own answer was: 'Morisot is a woman, and therefore capricious. Unfortunately she is like Eve who bites the apple and then gives up on it too soon. Too bad, since she bites so well!'

De Charry was not the first to seek to explain Morisot's manner of working by the fact of her femininity. In 1877 Georges Rivière had called her talent 'so charming and feminine', and in the same year, Philippe Burty, a consistently supportive critic, compared her use of pastel with that of the eighteenth-century pastellist Rosalba Carriera in an attempt to create an essential link between the work of the two female artists. She was often compared to Mary Cassatt, whom she was said to outstrip in 'femininity'. In later years, Impressionism itself was claimed by some critics to be a style suited to the 'superficiality' of a woman's temperament. Teodor de Wyzewa, for example, claimed that the marks made by Impressionist painters were expressive of qualities intrinsic to women. He saw the use of bright and clear tones as a parallel to the lightness, the fresh clarity, and the superficial elegance which make up a woman's vision, and declared: 'Only a woman has the right to rigorously practise the Impressionist system, she alone can limit her effort to the translation of impressions.' He believed that Morisot's greatest merit lay in offering 'an original vision which is entirely feminine'. Other critics have perpetuated this interpretation. In his introduction to the catalogue of her first one-woman exhibition, held at the Boussod and Valadon Gallery in 1892, Gustave Geffroy called hers '... a delicate painting which is a feminine painting', and in the same year Georges Lecomte, Pissarro's friend and biographer, maintained that the Impressionist style was more suited than any other to allow this delicate feminine temperament to develop. In 1907 the critic Claude Roger-Marx wrote that the term 'Impressionist' itself implied a manner of perceiving and recording which corresponded well to the hypersensitivity and nervousness of women.

Such claims form part of the dominant nineteenth-century view of femininity. They neither recognize the fact that most of the Impressionists were male, nor do they acknowledge the variety of different ways, from the naturalism of Louise Abbema (Pl. 49) to the symbolism of Virginie Demont-Breton (Pl. 50), in which other contemporary women artists worked. To seek to explain the stylistic characteristics of Impressionism with reference to 'femininity' is to imply that Morisot did not exert a sufficient degree of conscious control over her working practices, and that her 'style' is the unconscious expression of self. In the case of her male colleagues, however, due recognition is given to their deliberate exploration of certain aesthetic and political choices, which resulted in a particular way of working. A comparison of Morisot's work with that of contemporary work by her male associates indicates the absurdity of attributing her style to her 'femininity'. Such paintings as Monet's *Wild Poppies* (1873) (Pl. 53) share with Morisot's work that lightness of touch, degree of tonal clarity, and use of painterly brushmarks which are seen as the hallmark of the Impressionist method. These characteristics were part of a conscious strategy to free the paintings from the high degree of finish, disciplined tonal modelling, and emphasis on drawing so prized by academic painters.

A letter to Edma of 1875, written from the Isle of Wight, indicates vividly the difficulties that Morisot confronted in painting *en plein air*:

> My work is going badly.... It is always the same story: I don't know where to start. I made an attempt in a field, but the moment I had set up my easel more than fifty boys and girls were swarming about me, shouting and gesticulating. ... On a boat one has another kind of difficulty. Everything sways, there is an infernal lapping of water; one has the sun and the wind to cope with, the boats change position every minute, etc.... The view from my window is pretty to look at, but not to paint. Views from above are almost always incomprehensible; as a result of all this I am not doing much ...

In what she once described as a 'pitched battle' with her canvases, Morisot shows that she was fully aware of the difficulty implicit in attempting to render the immediate on canvas.

A painting shown at the second Impressionist exhibition, *Hanging the Laundry out to Dry* (Pl. 38) reveals how Morisot adopted a practice of using the *tache* (colour patch), indicating forms with a minimum of drawing, and allowing the light-coloured canvas ground to show through in many areas. It blurs the distinction between a sketch and a finished painting to an extent that most critics who commented on it found noteworthy. In its composition, with the horizontal fence cutting off the pictorial space from that of the viewer, it is notably less traditional than Monet's view of the same area *The Seine at Argenteuil* (Pl. 54), shown at the same exhibition. Morisot may have been in a position to show uncompromising paintings like this because she did not have to sell, and so did not feel obliged to make her work acceptable to dealers.

Critics hostile to the exhibition in 1876 regarded Morisot, no less than Degas, Renoir, and Monet, as representative of a 'revolutionary' movement in painting. Albert Wolff launched a fierce attack in *Le Figaro*, claiming: 'This is the revolutionary school, and France—which one accuses rightly or wrongly of loving revolutionaries—seems to me to like them less today in art than in politics.' Other conservative critics, such as Charles Bigot, were equally condemnatory, believing that the artists had formulated a system which had entrapped them. By contrast, critics who viewed the exhibition with enthusiasm tended to think that the work produced did not yet live up to the theory which underpinned it. As Morisot noted to an aunt, the critics' response was largely determined by the political persuasion of the papers for whom they wrote: 'If you read any Paris newspapers, among others the *Figaro*, which is so popular with the respectable public, you must know that I am one of a group of artists who are holding a show of their own, and you must also have seen how little

43. Berthe Morisot. *Summer (Young Woman by a Window)*. 1878. Oil on canvas, 76 × 61 cm. (29⅞ × 24 in.)
Montpellier, Musée Fabre

44. Berthe Morisot. *Winter (Woman with a Muff)*. 1880. Oil on canvas, 73.5 × 58.5 cm. (29 × 23 in.) Dallas, Museum of Art, Gift of the Meadows Foundation Inc.

45. Alfred Stevens. *Summer*.
c. 1878. Oil on canvas, 118 × 59.5
cm. (46½ × 23⅜ in.) Williamstown,
Mass., Sterling and Francine Clark
Art Institute

46. Edouard
Manet. *Autumn*.
1881. Oil on
canvas, 73 × 51
cm. (28¾ × 20⅛
in.) Nancy, Musée
des Beaux Arts

47. Berthe Morisot. *Lady at her Toilet. c.* 1875. Oil on canvas, 60.3 × 80.4 cm. (23¾ × 31½ in.) Chicago, The Art Institute, the Stickney Fund

48. Berthe Morisot. *The Wet Nurse Angele Feeding Julie Manet.* 1880. Oil on canvas, 50 × 61 cm. (19¾ × 24 in.) Private collection

49. Louise Abbema. *Luncheon in the Conservatory*. 1877. Oil on canvas, 194 × 308 cm. (78 × 123 in.) Pau, Musée des Beaux Arts

favour this exhibition enjoys in the eyes of the gentlemen of the press. On the other hand, we have been praised in the radical papers, but these you do not read. Anyway, we are being discussed, and we are so proud of it that we are all very happy.'

Both sectors of opinion agreed that Morisot was a key member of the group, and as the work of other members of the original group began increasingly to diverge, she came to be seen, as Paul Mantz described her in *Le Temps* in 1877, as 'the one real Impressionist'. Mantz declared that her painting had 'all the frankness of an improvisation; it does truly give the idea of an ''impression'' registered by a sincere eye and rendered again by a hand completely without trickery.' The lightly worked, freely brushed surfaces of her canvases continued to evoke comments of this sort. The adjectives 'charming', 'delicate', 'sensitive', or, in the hostile criticism of J.-K. Huysmans, 'hysterical', recur in the criticism and show that Morisot's femininity was never forgotten, and was always seen to be the origin of her works' appearance.

It was in the last decade of her life that Morisot's work moved increasingly away from the emphasis on observation and *plein-air* painting characteristic of her early years, and the evocative power hinted at by Mirbeau in 1886 became something she chose to emphasize. Her work process resembled more closely the

50. Virginie Demont-Breton. *Fisherman's Wife Going to Bathe her Children*. Salon 1881. Engraving. Present whereabouts and dimensions of original unknown

Virginie Demont-Breton 1881

51. Berthe Morisot. *Peasant Hanging the Washing.* 1881. Oil on canvas, 46 × 67 cm. (18⅛ × 26⅜ in.) Copenhagen, Ny Carlsberg Glyptotek

52. Berthe Morisot. *In the Dining Room*. 1886. Oil on canvas, 61.3 × 50 cm. (24⅛ × 19¾ in.) Washington D.C., National Gallery of Art, Chester Dale Collection

traditional practice of utilizing preliminary sketches and sometimes oil studies as stages in the planning of a composition. Like Renoir, her close friend in these years, she sometimes produced work that was deliberately more monumental and symbolic than the paintings of the impressionist years. Such a painting was *The Cherry Tree* (Pl. 55), for which several preliminary studies exist. Morisot began by sketching her daughter Julie standing on a ladder picking fruit, while her cousin Jeannie Gobillard, Yves's daughter, handed her a basket. A water-colour version of this early compositional arrangement also exists (Pl. 56), and Morisot produced pastel studies of both individual figures. The original studies were made in the garden of the rented house in Mézy where Morisot and her family spent the summer of 1891. During the following winter, working in her

53. Claude Monet. *Wild Poppies.* 1873. Oil on canvas, 50 × 65 cm. (19¾ × 25⅝ in.) Paris, Musée d'Orsay

54. Claude Monet. *The Seine at Argenteuil*. 1875. Oil on canvas, 59.7 × 81.3 cm. (23½ × 32 in.) San Francisco, Museum of Modern Art, Bequest of Mrs Henry Potter Russell 74.4

studio in the Rue de Villejust, Morisot returned to the theme, employing a professional model to pose for the figure on the ladder. After the death of Eugène in 1892, Morisot moved to the Rue Wéber. It was here, in the winter of 1892–93, that she completed the final version of *The Cherry Tree*, using another professional model to pose for the figure on the ladder. This sequential exploration of a single theme over a period of almost two years is in marked contrast to the more immediate and direct method of working of the 1870s. The careful organization of the composition, the emphasis on flowing lines, and its suggestion of fertility and the natural cycle are a marked departure from the observation of a particular moment suggested in the earlier paintings.

In 1891 Morisot's close friend Stéphane Mallarmé said in an interview: 'I think ... that there should be only allusion. The contemplation of objects, the image emanating from the dreams which the objects excite, this is poetry ... To suggest, that is the dream....' Morisot's later work has much in common with this ideal of suggestiveness. The sketchiness of handling which had characterized her painting since the 1870s broadened into sweeping painterly brushmarks, and the debate about the sketch versus the finished painting, so important in the Impressionist years, was superseded by a concern with the evocation of mood and atmosphere.

55. Berthe Morisot. *The Cherry Tree*. 1893. Oil on canvas, 152 × 85 cm. (59¾ × 33½ in.) Paris, Private collection

56. Berthe Morisot. Study for '*The Cherry Tree*'. c. 1891. Watercolour on paper, 44 × 27.5 cm. (17¼ × 11 in.) New York, Private collection

4 *The Painting of Bourgeois Life*

When Charles Baudelaire called for a painting that expressed the 'heroism of modern life', he cast the artist as the passionate *flâneur* who sets 'up house in the heart of the multitude, amid the ebb and flow of movement, in the midst of the fugitive and the infinite'. The *flâneur* was to inhabit the world as though it were his own: 'To be away from home and yet to feel oneself everywhere at home.... The lover of life makes the whole world his family, just like the lover of the fair sex who builds up his family from all the beautiful women that he has ever found ....' He recommended 'speedy execution' to capture 'the daily metamorphosis of external things' and 'rapidity of movement' in the creation of the 'sketch of manners' and 'the depiction of bourgeois life'.

The artist that Baudelaire constructed is one who is in control of his movements, his money, his morality, and most firmly, his masculinity. An independent, free-wheeling agent, he makes the modern city his territory, commanding it with his gaze, unwatched but watching, ever vigilant. It was the spectacle of modernity, fiercely urban in quality, and characterized as 'the ephemeral, the fugitive, the contingent', which in Baudelaire's schema provided the appropriate subject matter for modern painting. Such a model for art and artist was pitted consciously and strategically against the prevailing concerns of the Academy with its continuing promotion of historical and mythological narratives as the subjects most worthy of art, and of smoothly finished surfaces, subtle modulations of tone, and complex formal compositions as the most fitting means through which an appropriately grand and uplifting national painting could be expressed.

But what were the implications of Baudelaire's widely publicized injunction for the woman artist, to whom the city was a forbidden and forbidding territory, inaccessible to her by virtue of both her class and gender? Heavily chaperoned, corseted, and formally dressed, she could not become the unobtrusive observer/participator of the pageant of modern life as played out in the cafés-concerts, dance halls, and street life of the growing city. The world could not become her

57. Marie Bracquemond. *The Umbrellas*. 1882. Charcoal and white paint on paper, 25 × 38 cm. (10 × 15 in.) Paris, Musée du Louvre, Cabinet des Dessins

58. Honoré Daumier. *The Blue Stockings*. 1844. Lithograph, 23.3 × 19 cm. (9⅛ × 7½ in.) Paris, Bibliothèque Nationale

59. Mary Cassatt. *Mother about to Wash her Sleepy Child*. 1880. Oil on canvas, 100 × 65 cm. (39⅜ × 25⅝ in.) Los Angeles, County Museum of Art, Bequest of Mrs Fred Hathaway Bixby

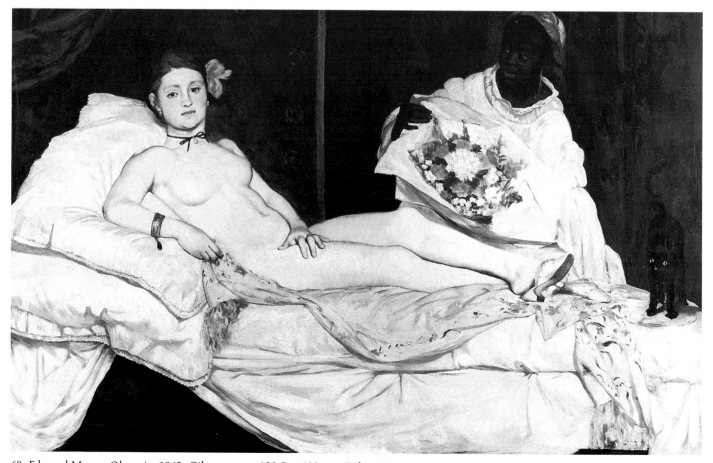

60. Edouard Manet. *Olympia*. 1863. Oil on canvas, 130.5 × 190 cm. (51½ × 75 in.) Paris, Musée d'Orsay

61. William Adolphe Bouguereau. *Mother and Child (The Rest)*. 1879. Oil on canvas, 164 × 117 cm. (64¾ × 46¼ in.) Cleveland, Ohio, The Cleveland Museum of Art, Hinman B. Hurlbut Collection

home, and the city could not function as a site across which she could express her mobility and define her sexuality. On the rare occasion when she does represent the city, with its sprawling crowds and free mixing of classes, it retains the air of a studio study, tightly constructed and carefully composed as in Marie Bracquemond's *The Umbrellas* (Pl. 57).

Artists like Morisot and Cassatt were acutely aware of the ways in which their male colleagues negotiated the problem of representing 'modernity' and of the debates and arguments which informed their methods. But the problem for them of representing 'modern life' had to be confronted from the restricted arena in which they, as women, were allowed to operate. This was the arena of the home, the private sphere widely believed in the nineteenth century to be 'naturally' the sphere of women, and increasingly gaining its meaning in the second half of the century as defined against the growing city, the site of luxury and commerce. There were women in the city of course, and many of the male artists depicted them, but they were of a class and character far removed from the world of the bourgeois woman artist. There is no place for the woman artist in Baudelaire's scheme of things. 'Woman' for him, and for so many of his contemporaries, fluctuates between being 'a divinity, a star ... a kind of idol, stupid perhaps, but dazzling and bewitching', and 'a perfect image of the savagery that lurks in the midst of civilization', and it was this creature which the male artist was to 'observe' and depict. The image of the *flâneur*, the dominant model for the 'avant-garde' artist at the moment of the birth of such a concept, is predicated on the notion that the artist be male.

Within nineteenth-century ideas on women's nature, it was difficult to accommodate the woman artist, or the literary or professional woman. Daumier had in 1844 represented the intellectual woman as an uncaring wife and mother in his satirical caricatures of *The Blue Stockings* published in *Le Charivari* (Pl. 58). Morisot's close friend Renoir had views on women artists and intellectuals which were typically conservative: 'I consider women writers, lawyers and politicians [such as] George Sand, Mme Adam and other bores as monsters and nothing but five-legged calves. The woman artist is merely ridiculous, but I am in favour of the female singer and dancer.' Renoir adhered firmly to the dominant *femme au foyer* doctrine. With the consolidation of bourgeois society in this period women's roles became increasingly circumscribed. Legitimate womanhood could be expressed through motherhood, symbolized by the powerful image of the Virgin Mary and reinterpreted in the late nineteenth century as the 'Modern Madonna' (Pls. 61, 62) or through the prostitute, regarded as the only other possible outlet for a 'useful' female sexuality (Pl. 60). The intellectual woman having abdicated from her 'true' vocation was even associated with the prostitute. Renoir's son Jean, in his anecdotal biography of his father, recounted that one gentleman visitor was so outraged by the works on auction at the Hôtel Drouot in 1875 that he called Morisot a *gourgandine*, a streetwalker.

The family, as an institution, was widely believed to be women's responsibility, and creative expression for the vast majority of women of Morisot's class had to find its outlet in the home. For the mature Morisot, in many respects a conventional *haute-bourgeoise*, the home and the domestic garden or park were her domain. But unlike most women of her class who devoted themselves to the tasks of caring for and supporting families, supervising the home, engaging in charity work, executing intricate and highly skilled needlework, and socializing, Morisot turned her domestic situation into the overriding subject of more than twenty years of painting.

Within the Impressionist celebration of 'modernity', the domestic was elevated to a level of significance hitherto never accorded to it. The painting of scenes of contemporary life was not new in the late nineteenth century. Women had long specialized in the portrayal of everyday life, particularly domestic events, but such 'genre' paintings had been widely regarded in as disparaging a way as still life had been in the early and mid-nineteenth century. With the conscious rejection of historical narrative painting and large-scale figure compositions by avant-garde critics and artists, genre painting could be elevated to the 'painting of modern life' and proclaimed as the painting of the new age. The meaning of the depiction of everyday life, long the concern of genre painters, albeit with some didacticism, was transformed through an alteration of technique. For those late nineteenth-century Salon painters who used the conventions of photographic naturalism as a means of representing scenes from everyday life, the term 'genre painting' persisted, for example, to describe Marie Bashkirtseff's *The Meeting* (Pl. 64). Those who adopted Impressionist techniques to represent contemporary life, on the other hand, were seen by sympathetic critics and artists to be making an intervention against the restrictive subjects, styles, and meanings promoted by the Academy.

The most significant way in which women artists who identified with 'avant-garde' theories could heed the urgent call to contemporaneity by critics and artists was to focus on the world that surrounded them in the home. The portrayal of family life within the domestic setting, formed, understandably, the most important element in the iconography of all the women Impressionists, as the works of Marie Bracquemond and Mary Cassatt show (Pl. 59). Morisot's painting celebrates bourgeois womanhood in all its stages: from pregnancy (Pls. 14, 17), through the first months of motherhood (Pl. 15) through the years of caring. The world of women's labour very often forms the subject of her paintings. The bourgeois woman in her home would have been surrounded by other women, her family or paid servants. It is the daily rituals which comprised a women's world, sewing, nursing, and minding children, which Morisot so often represents.

Morisot rarely depicted men except for the few occasions when she represented her husband Eugène, sometimes with their child Julie in a number of rare treatments of the *paternité* theme. These show father and daughter usually engaged in some activity together, on one occasion playing a board game (Pl. 66), on another reading or sketching (Pl. 67).

It was the theme of *maternité* which had much greater currency in the France of the Third Republic, especially in the decades following the Franco-Prussian

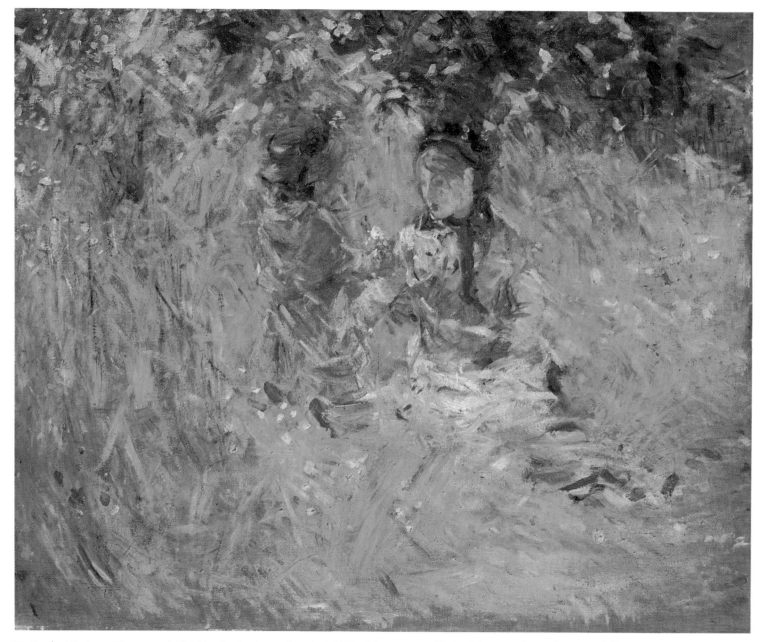

62. Berthe Morisot. *Woman and Child in the Garden at Bougival.* 1882. Oil on canvas, 59.6 × 73 cm. (23½ × 28¾ in.) Cardiff, National Museum of Wales

63. Berthe Morisot. *Woman and Child in a Garden*. 1884. Oil on canvas, 59 × 72 cm. (23¼ × 28⅜ in.) Edinburgh, National Gallery of Scotland

64. Marie Bashkirtseff. *The Meeting*. 1884. Oil on canvas, 193 × 177 cm. (77 × 71 in.) Paris, Musée du Louvre

65. Marie Bracquemond. *Tea Time*. 1880. Oil on canvas, 81.5 × 61.5 cm. (32⅛ × 24¼ in.) Paris, Musée du Petit Palais

66. Berthe Morisot. *Eugène Manet and his Daughter at Bougival.* 1881. Oil on canvas, 73 × 92 cm. (28¾ × 36¼ in.) Paris, Private collection

67. Berthe Morisot. *Eugène Manet and his Daughter in the Garden.* 1883. Oil on canvas, 60 × 73 cm. (23⅝ × 28¾ in.) Paris, Private collection

War in which France had suffered enormous casualties. Although Morisot painted images of women and children all her life, her compositions rarely recall well-known paintings of the Virgin and Child, as was then the vogue, being, on the whole, less formally composed. One exception to this is the relatively traditional composition of the *Portrait of Mme Boursier and her Daughter*, Morisot's cousin and her child (Pl. 73). It was more usual for her paintings to produce the effect of being quickly recorded, transient moments, the traditional theme apparently transformed by the method of its representation into a 'painting of modern life'. This is particularly true of the many watercolours that Morisot executed, in which, like many of her colleagues, she strove to create the effect of casual arrangements and immediacy (Pl. 15). What remains intact in these images, albeit disguised under the cloak of naturalist reportage, is the traditional association of women with children, the domestic, the 'natural'. But Morisot's work avoids the cloying sentimentality or overt moralizing of many of the paintings on this theme. In some of her early compositions of women and children, usually modelled by her sisters, their children, and paid nurses, each appears to inhabit a world of her own meditations. In *In a Villa at the Seaside* (Pl. 35), for example, the independence of the child is asserted by her apparent obliviousness to her guardian. In *Woman and Child in a Garden* (Pl. 63) there is even a physical barrier, created by the tree between the figures. Other versions of the theme show women and children resting and playing (Pl. 62), with the woman occasionally deeply absorbed in her needlework.

As well as being a professional painter Morisot was a committed mother and never seems to have believed that the two roles were incompatible for herself. Because of her wealth and privilege on the one hand and her exceptionally supportive husband on the other, she was able to integrate these two aspects of her life without any apparent difficulty. By contrast, Marie Bracquemond, who had neither Morisot's wealth nor an encouraging partner, gave up painting when she was still relatively young because of the domestic friction which her work provoked.

Morisot's only daughter, Julie, became her favourite model, and it was through drawing and painting that she recorded her physical development from infancy through girlhood and early adolescence. Morisot was able to hire a wet nurse to breast-feed her baby, which left her free to paint, on one occasion showing Julie being nursed (Pl. 48), on another sitting on her nurse's lap (Pl. 68). During the 1880s and early 1890s Morisot painted and drew frequently from Julie, often placing her in the garden with a young companion. From 1881 to 1884 the family spent their summers in their holiday home at Bougival, and Julie, with friends, cousins, nurses, or her father is repeatedly portrayed (Pl. 66). A drypoint of 1887 shows Morisot drawing with her daughter peering attentively over her shoulder (Pl. 70), while a drawing of 1889 shows the now ten-year-old girl being taught to embroider (Pl. 71). The adolescent Julie is also represented, on one occasion with her greyhound Laertes, a gift from Mallarmé (Pl. 69).

Morisot's representation of bourgeois life was not restricted to the portrayal of family life alone, but the settings of her paintings were more often than not in, or in the vicinity of, the home. 'Modernity' meant something different for women than it did for men. The world of the boulevards and the life of the *demi-monde* being inappropriate and inaccessible as subject matter for women artists, the contemporary world which they represented is that which they experienced. Both Eva Gonzalès and Mary Cassatt painted scenes of the theatres of Paris where grandly attired *haut-bourgeois* women would occupy private boxes with their families and friends (Pls. 72, 74), but Morisot's modern life subjects are more suggestive than illustrative. Perhaps this is due to the very secluded life that she led as a Frenchwoman of a particular class. She never painted the theatres and music halls of the modern city, and the settings for her subjects are only hinted at, often by the titles of her paintings. Morisot set up 'scenes from modern life' in her own home, fulfilling thereby the demands of 'relevance' while maintaining her position as the *femme au foyer*. In *At the Ball* (Pl. 40), for example, a young woman dressed in an evening gown is seated in what seems to be the interior of the Morisot home (this is indicated by the indoor garden behind her head, which appears in other paintings), and it is only the title and elaborate costume that provide any indication that this may be a painting of a woman at a ball.

Like many of her male colleagues, Morisot executed a number of paintings on the theme of the woman at her toilette (Pl. 77). The association of women and mirrors is a traditional one, but whereas in academic painting it appeared in the mythic context of Venus at the mirror, or in the image of Vanitas, symbolizing vain earthly beauty, in the work of the Impressionists, these mythic associations are projected onto contemporary women. The private daily ritual of combing hair, bathing, dressing, or applying make-up became a popular subject in the 1870s and 1880s. Although the specific narrative of traditional paintings is discarded, the projection of vanity onto women alone remains intact. (There are no images of men arranging their toilette in front of mirrors at this time.) This is not to say that artists, men or women, consciously saw such images as vehicles for the expression of female vanity, but it indicates why these images were made possible and deemed 'natural' within this context. Ideas about masculinity and femininity are produced within the systems of belief of their time, and it would be unreasonable to expect women to be able to stand outside of these. But whereas scenes of women at the toilette by male artists are often satirical like Manet's *Nana* (Pl. 75) or exposing like Degas's *Woman in a Tub* (Pl. 76), those by women are often gentle and sympathetic. In *Psyche* of 1876 (Pl. 42), a young woman dressed in white glances at her reflection in the *psyche*, or mirror, and the painting is an exploration of awakening sexuality and adolescent self-awareness, without any of the caricatural elements of some contemporary imagery. Some of Morisot's works on this theme do show the woman in a state of semi-undress as in *Lady at her Toilet* (Pl. 47), where Morisot's subject is in keeping with contemporary constructions of womanhood. It was widely thought at this time that the 'toilette' was for women the equivalent of painting for men. While the art of self-decoration was deemed appropriate to a suitably feminine sensibility,

68. Berthe Morisot. *Julie with her Nurse*. 1880. Oil on canvas, 73 × 60 cm. (29 × 24 in.) Ny Carlsberg Glyptotek, Copenhagen

69. Berthe Morisot. *Julie Manet and her Greyhound Laertes*. 1893. Oil on canvas, 73 × 80 cm. (29 × 31½ in.) Paris, Musée Marmottan

70. Berthe
Morisot. *Berthe
Morisot Drawing
with her
Daughter.* 1889.
Drypoint, 18.2 ×
13.6 cm. (7$\frac{1}{8}$ × 5$\frac{3}{8}$
in.) London,
British Museum,
Department of
Prints and
Drawings

71. Berthe Morisot. *Embroidery*.
1889. Pencil, 19 × 22 cm. (7½ × 8⅝
in.) Paris, Musée du Petit Palais

and to the role of women as attractive and appealing objects for male delectation,
the art of painting was regarded as 'masculine'. Paradoxically, what Morisot, the
committed painter, presents in these paintings is an image of femininity which is
entirely in keeping with the prescriptions for women of her time.

One small representation of this subject, the drawing *Before the Mirror*,
shows a seated woman, partially unclothed, arranging her hair in front of a
mirror (Pl. 78). It is possible that Morisot, working here on a small scale,
probably in a private sketchbook, felt free to handle the theme of the nude in a
modern life setting. For the most part, women were unwilling to tackle the
theme of the nude, inhibited as they were by their restricted training and by
current notions of decency.

72. Eva Gonzalès. *A Loge at the Théâtre des Italiens*. c. 1874. Oil on canvas, 98 × 130 cm. (38⅝ × 51⅛ in.) Paris, Musée d'Orsay

Baudelaire had been careful to replace the historical and mythological narrative material which had traditionally facilitated the representation of the naked female form with a new 'modern life' alternative: 'The nude—that darling of the artists, that necessary element of success—is just as frequent and necessary today as it was in the life of the ancients; in bed, for example, or in the bath, or in the anatomy theatre. The themes and resources of painting are equally abundant and varied; but there is a new element—modern beauty.' There was, therefore, no decrease in the popularity of the nude as a subject for art in the context of realist and naturalist debates. For Degas and Manet, the prostitute provided the means which allowed them to retain the naked female form as a subject for art while conforming to current notions of 'contemporaneity'. Manet's *Olympia* presented an image of the modern courtesan as unashamed and assertive, while Degas's many images of washing and bathing presented women as though unobserved—modern-day Susannahs with the elders displaced outside the canvas. Simultaneously, the mythic, idealized image of naked women continued to be popular, even within the Impressionist circle, as Renoir's *Nude in the Sunlight*, for instance, testifies.

There is no evidence to show that Morisot had any training in drawing from the naked model, but in the late 1880s and 1890s she executed a number of

73. Berthe Morisot. *Portrait of Mme Boursier and her Daughter*. 1874. Oil on canvas, 73 × 56.5 cm. (28¾ × 22¼ in.) New York, Brooklyn Museum, Museum Collection Fund

74. Mary Cassatt. *At the Opera*. 1880. Oil on canvas, 80 × 64.8 cm. (31½ × 25½ in.) Boston, Museum of Fine Arts, Charles Henry Hayden Fund

75. Edouard Manet. *Nana*. 1877. Oil on canvas, 154 × 115 cm. (60⅝ × 45¼ in.) Hamburg, Kunsthalle

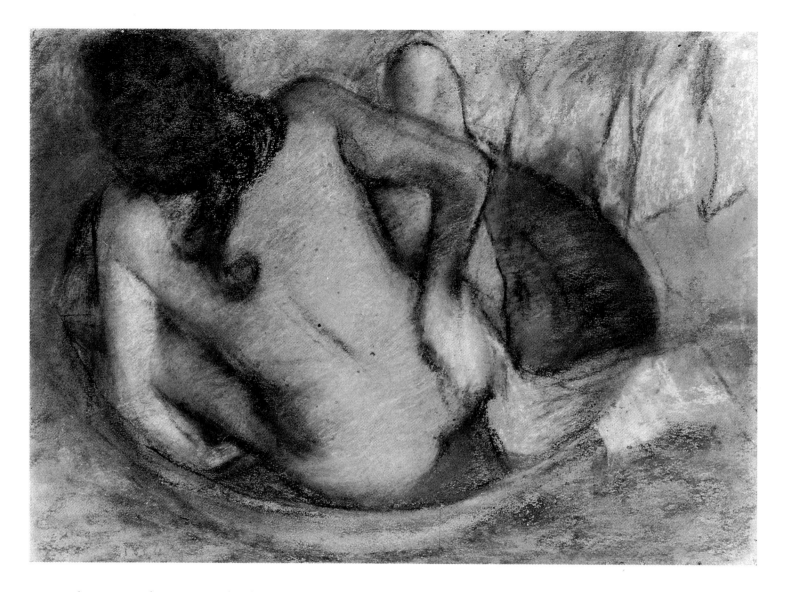

drawings and paintings of naked or semi-naked women in the idealized and generalized, often linear vein which also characterized Renoir's work. For Morisot, Baudelaire's injunction to locate the naked woman within a realistic context offered more limited opportunities than it did for her male colleagues. On one occasion she posed a professional model in the bathroom at the Rue de Villejust, executing a painting, a charcoal drawing, and a drypoint of this theme (Pl. 79). Most of her nudes were done in the last years of her life when she sought a more mythic and generalized pictorial language removed from the evocation of contemporary life. She executed a series of works on the traditionally pastoral theme of the naked shepherdess for example.

Morisot is an interesting case. A bourgeois woman who prided herself on her elegant and fashionable clothes, a mother and a wife who valued both these roles, a painter and colleague of the Impressionists, she was able to use her situation and her vision of the world to create a body of work, which, while indicating her tenacity and strength in being able to manipulate her circumstances to advantage, also reflected the dominant, often stereotypical constructions of femininity of her time.

76. Edgar Degas. *Woman in a Tub.* c. 1884. Pastel on paper, 45 × 65 cm. (17¾ × 25⅝ in.) Glasgow, The Burrell Collection, Glasgow Art Gallery and Museum

77. Berthe Morisot. *Young Woman Powdering her Face.* 1877. Oil on canvas, 46 × 38 cm. (18 x 16 in.) Paris, Musée d'Orsay

78. Berthe Morisot. *Before the Mirror*. 1890. Pencil, 30 × 20 cm. (11⅞ × 7⅞ in.) Paris, Musée du Louvre, Cabinet des Dessins

79. Berthe Morisot. *Nude Seen in Back View*. 1889. Drypoint, 13 × 19.2 cm. (5⅛ × 7½ in.) London, British Museum, Department of Prints and Drawings

The Evocation of Place

From the early 1850s, when the family first moved to Paris, Morisot lived in a number of locations within a confined area. Until her death in 1895, all her Paris residences were within Passy. This was a village which had already acquired its name in the thirteenth century, and had been a fashionable spa in the eighteenth century, when it was also renowned as the residence of Le Riche de la Popelinière, a patron of painters, among them Georges de la Tour and Chardin, writers including Jean-Jacques Rousseau, and musicians such as Rameau. By the mid-nineteenth century, its population had begun to grow rapidly, and by 1856 it had doubled in size in a decade. In 1859 it became the sixteenth *arrondissement* of Paris, as part of Baron Haussmann's administrative programme, and its character gradually changed as the population grew, although its village-like atmosphere continued to be prized by local residents until well into the twentieth century. Georges Lecomte described it as 'a picturesque and Parisian village, separated from the tumult of Paris, because the Bois de Boulogne, so close to my home, is like a personal park where, among the mighty trees and the calm waters of its lakes, I walk and meditate agreeably.' Because of its situation, so close to the Bourse and the business centre of Paris, and because of its excellent transportation links to the Gare Saint-Lazare, Passy became a suburb developed in emulation of the suburbs of London, where prosperous businessmen established their family homes in what could still be seen as semi-country, while keeping their places of work in the city centre. This ensured its continuing growth, and its population increased tenfold during the forty years Morisot lived there. It was an area that numbered many prominent figures among its residents, including Victor Hugo, who declared: 'Paris is the capital of France and the sixteenth *arrondissement* is the capital of Paris.'

The Morisots lived first in the Rue de Moulins (now the Rue Scheffer), which had in the eighteenth century been the site of three windmills, and marked one of the boundaries of the village, but they then moved to the Rue Franklin, named after Benjamin Franklin, who lived in Passy between 1777 and 1785. This is close

80. Berthe Morisot. *View of Paris from the Trocadéro*. 1872. Oil on canvas, 46.1 × 81.5 cm. (18⅛ × 32⅛ in.) Santa Barbara, Santa Barbara Museum of Art, gift of Mrs Hugh N. Kirkland

81. Berthe Morisot. *Boats—Entry to the Midina in the Isle of Wight.* 1875. Watercolour on paper, 19 × 17.5 cm. (7½ × 7 in.) Cambridge, Mass., The Fogg Art Museum

to the park and Trocadéro Palace, built for the 1878 Universal Exhibition. The
Morisots' home was near to the Pont d'Iéna, a bridge built across the Seine
during Napoleon I's reign, to commemorate his victory over the Prussians, and it
was depicted by Morisot in her 1867 Salon submission, *The Seine below the Pont
d'Iéna* (Pl. 29). The rural character of the location had still not fundamentally
changed when Gauguin painted the same bridge eight years later (Pl. 82).

In 1872 Morisot painted a view of Paris from the site of the old Trocadéro
Gardens, *View of Paris from the Trocadéro* (Pl. 80), looking down over the lawns
to the Pont d'Iéna below, and across the river to the city on the horizon. The
dome of the Hôtel des Invalides is prominent, with to its right, the cupola of the
Panthéon, and to its left, the towers of Saint-Sulpice. Also identifiable are the
towers of Notre-Dame, in the centre of the painting, and to its left, the towers of
Saint-Clotilde. The open area indicated beyond the bridge is the Champ de Mars,
later to be the site of the Eiffel Tower. The curve of green lawn and the railing
establishes a sense of the distance of the city from the Trocadéro Gardens.

82. Paul Gauguin. *The Seine at
Pont d'Iéna*. 1875. Oil on canvas,
65 × 92 cm. (25⅝ × 36¼ in.) Paris,
Musée d'Orsay

83. Edouard Manet. *The Exposition Universelle, Paris, 1867.* 1867. Oil on canvas, 108 × 196.5 cm. (42½ × 77⅜ in.) Oslo, National Gallery

Guidebooks recommended this vantage point, but the women in Morisot's painting are oblivious to the view, and only the little girl is shown looking towards the dense cluster of buildings. The fashionably dressed women, probably posed by Morisot's sisters, are identifiable as Passy residents, whose tranquil surroundings were detached from the city below them. This painting is often compared to Manet's *The Exposition Universelle, Paris 1867* (Pl. 83), but Manet's lower vantage point and collection of urban types represents the complexity and diversity of the expanding city, with the exhibition itself bringing the city into the suburbs, whereas in Morisot's painting the city is alien and apart from the women. Both the oil painting and the watercolour *On the Balcony* (Pl. 18), evoke a similar sense of detachment from the distant city. The woman represented in this painting does not look out towards the Invalides, but at the child beside her, and the railing effectively separates the world of Passy from that of Paris.

During the 1850s and 1860s the development of the railways had made the Normandy coast newly accessible to Parisian visitors. The *trains de plaisir* (tourist trains) made the journey quick, and the seaside resorts soon became places which, as the English writer Henry Blackburn noted, combined 'the refinements, pleasures and ''distractions'' of Paris with northern breezes'. The Morisot family were among many others of their class for whom this ease of access meant that summers could be spent along the Channel coast. Morisot made regular visits to popular places, such as Beuzeval on the Normandy coast, which she visited in 1864 and again in 1879, Petites Dalles, near Fécamp, where

84. Berthe Morisot. *The Village at Maurecourt.* 1873. Pastel on paper, 47 × 72 cm. (18½ × 28⅜ in.) Private collection

85. Berthe Morisot. *In the Garden at Maurecourt*. 1884. Oil on canvas, 54 × 65 cm. (21¼ × 25⅝ in.) Toledo, Ohio, The Toledo Museum of Art, Gift of Edward Drummond Libbey

she spent some time in 1867 and 1873, Fécamp itself, where she visited Edma and her husband Adolphe Pontillon in 1873 and again in 1874, and Cherbourg, where she spent three months with Edma in 1871.

The development of the Normandy resorts was accompanied by a proliferation of guidebooks, which used small wood engravings as illustrations to prepare visitors for their journeys, offering an easily assimilated landscape of tourism, but these were not the views which Morisot chose to depict. It is characteristic of her concern with the domestic that she rarely showed the scenic features of these places, the subjects of paintings by artists such as Boudin, Jongkind, and Monet. When in Fécamp, for example, she did not choose to represent the cliffs and the dramatic interface between land and sea of that

86. Claude Monet. *Calm Weather, Fécamp.* 1881. Oil on canvas, 60 × 72.5 cm. (23⅝ × 28½ in.) Basel, Fondation Rudolf Staechelin

87. Eugène Boudin. *Jetty and Wharf at Trouville*. 1863. Oil on canvas, 34.6 × 57.8 cm. (13⅝ × 22⅞ in.) Washington D.C., National Gallery of Art, Collection of Mr and Mrs Paul Mellon

88. Alfred Sisley. *The Furrows*. 1873. Oil on canvas, 45.5 × 64.5 cm. (18 × 25½ in.) Copenhagen, Ny Carlsberg Glyptotek

89. Berthe Morisot. *In the Wheatfield.* 1875. Oil on canvas, 46 × 69 cm. (18⅛ × 27⅛ in.) Paris, Musée d'Orsay

90. Berthe Morisot. *The Quay at Bougival.* 1883. Oil on canvas, 55 × 46 cm. (21⅝ × 18⅛ in.) Oslo, National Gallery

91. Provost. *The Inauguration of the Bougival Bridge, 7 November 1858.* Paris, Bibliothèque Nationale

92. Anonymous.
Morisot's Studio.
c. 1890.
Photograph. Paris,
Collection
Sirot-Angel

93. W. Measom,
after Gustave
Janet. *The Bois de
Boulogne (Grande
Cascade).* 1859.
Wood engraving,
38.8 × 51.7 cm.
(15¼ × 20⅜ in.)
Paris, Musée
Carnavalet

94. Charles
Marville. *The Bois
de Boulogne.*
1858. Photograph,
36.2 × 49.8 cm.
(14¼ × 19⅜ in.)
Paris, Bibliothèque
Nationale

95. Berthe Morisot. *Girl in a Boat, with Geese.* 1889. Oil on canvas, 65.5 × 54.6 cm. (25¾ × 21½ in.) Washington D.C., National Gallery of Art, Ailsa Mellon Bruce Collection

96. Berthe Morisot. *Carriage in the Bois de Boulogne, Allée des Poteaux.* c. 1889. Watercolour on paper, 28.9 × 20.7 cm. (11⅜ × 8⅛ in.) Oxford, Ashmolean Museum

stretch of the Normandy coastline (Pl. 86) but concentrated in *In a Villa at the Seaside* (Pl. 35) on the curious timber architecture of the villa and the figures seated on the balcony. During her visit to Cherbourg she painted the watercolour *Woman and Child Seated in a Field* (Pl. 15), where the townscape appears in the background, separated from the two figures in a manner akin to that of the Paris views, which suggests the containment and enclosure of the nineteenth-century women's world.

The development of tourism in seaside towns in Brittany followed the pattern established earlier in Normandy. The town of Lorient on the Atlantic coast had recently begun receiving an influx of Parisian visitors when Morisot painted *The Harbour at Lorient* (Pl. 22). The fashionably dressed figure with her parasol, posed by Edma, is an urban accent in a rustic scene, a visitor enjoying the delights of the small fishing port. The depiction of the landscape of tourism was an extension of Baudelaire's call for contemporaneity in subject matter. Morisot's painting indicates that she shared the view expressed by Eugène Boudin, Monet's teacher, who often painted the tourist population in Normandy (Pl. 87). In 1868 Boudin asked a fellow resident of Le Havre, M. Martin: 'The peasants have their painters of predilection: Millet, Jacque, Breton, and this is good; but between ourselves these middle-class men and women, walking on the pier toward the setting sun, have they no right to be fixed on canvas, *to be brought to light?*'

Morisot's vision of the countryside is always that of a town dweller, a transient visitor rather than a permanent resident. Her brief sojourns in a variety of locations often led to a struggle to find and realize suitable motifs, and she shared the self-doubts often expressed by her colleagues Monet and Pissarro at the enormity of the problems posed by attempting to record passing effects of light and movement. On the Isle of Wight in 1875, for example, when she painted the watercolour *Boats—Entry to the Midina in the Isle of Wight* (Pl. 81), she described the difficulties of trying to render the 'extraordinary life and movement' she saw on the island in a letter to Edma, and added self-deprecat-ingly: 'It is the prettiest place for painting—if one had any talent.'

Like her colleagues, Morisot did not seek spectacular or even notably picturesque effects as subjects in the 1870s. Her pastel showing *The Village at Maurecourt* (Pl. 84) of 1873, exhibited at the first Impressionist exhibition, is characteristic of the Île-de-France landscapes, which Monet, Sisley (Pl. 88), and Pissarro also painted frequently. Edma and her husband lived in the hamlet of Maurecourt, in the Vexin valley, and Morisot spent part of three consecutive summers there. She returned to the village on many later occasions, often painting Edma's children in the Pontillons' garden (Pl. 85). This pastel shows the hamlet, a cluster of houses in an empty plain stretching to the river bank in the distance. The scene appears desolate, without any figures to enliven it, and the medium of pastel is used without any of the references to an eighteenth-century tradition, denoting grace and elegance, which often characterized pastels of the time.

Morisot also painted at Gennevilliers, where the Manet family had a property, in the mid-1870s. Gennevilliers is situated on a plain on a loop of the river Seine, midway between Asniéres and Argenteuil, six miles northwest of Paris. It is the area of France most closely associated with the development of Impressionist landscape painting in the 1870s, when Monet and Renoir were working at Argenteuil and were visited by Manet (Pl. 54). Morisot's *Hanging the Laundry out to Dry* (Pl. 38) declares this landscape's semi-urban aspect. As T. J. Clark has noted, a character in a contemporary *opéra-bouffe, Les Environs de Paris*, Monsieur Bartaval, had described his disillusionment with precisely such environs of Paris as Gennevilliers: 'When I set off I said to myself: And there, I shall have some air, some sun and greenery ... Oh, yes, greenery! Instead of cornflowers and poppies, great prairies covered with old clothes and detachable collars ... laundresses everywhere and not a single shepherdess ... factories instead of cottages ... too much sun ... no shade ... and to cap it all, great red brick chimneys giving out black smoke which poisons the lungs and makes you cough!' Morisot's motif is unashamedly 'modern', as it is in *In the Wheatfield* (Pl. 89) of 1875, also painted at Gennevilliers, which shows a landscape at the edge of urban development. The farmworker in the fields is juxtaposed against encroaching suburban and industrial sprawl. In many ways Passy, situated at the edge of the newly developed and planted Bois de Boulogne, was more of a retreat from the city than the harsh industrial reality of the Gennevilliers plain, with its smoking factory chimneys and its fields watered from the main collector sewer of Paris.

Morisot and her family spent the summers of the early 1880s in a rented house at Bougival, a bathing place on the Seine where Monet, Renoir, and Pissarro had painted before the Franco-Prussian War. Here she painted *The Quay at Bougival* (Pl. 90), one of the rare occasions on which she departed from her usual practice of painting her family, and turned instead to a view of the buildings lining the quay alongside the river (Pl. 91). Bougival was only twenty minutes by train from the Gare Saint-Lazare, and had long been viewed as an artists' colony. For Morisot it combined the advantage of accessibility with the attractions of the landscape and of the large garden of the rented house.

In 1890 and 1891 Morisot and her family stayed in a spacious rented house in the village of Mézy, on the Seine close to Meulan. Morisot had a studio in the loft, with fine views over the plateau of Le Gibet and the Seine valley, but she preferred to concentrate her attention on the view nearer to hand, and painted and drew Julie and her cousins and friends playing in the garden and orchard of the house. *The Cherry Tree* (Pls. 55, 56) was begun in the orchard.

In 1881 Morisot and her husband bought land in the Rue de Villejust in Passy, close to the Arc de Triomphe, but also closer to the Bois de Boulogne than her previous homes. By 1883 they were able to move into their newly built house, where Morisot lived for the next decade. The *salon* served as her studio, as photographs indicate (Pl. 92), and now the Bois itself became an extension to her private garden, as it did for so many Passy dwellers during the week. The Bois de Boulogne had changed entirely since Louis-Philippe's reign, when, as the playwright Victorien Sardou wrote, the surroundings were 'waste grounds ...,

97. Berthe Morisot. *Lady with a Parasol Sitting in a Park*. 1885. Watercolour on paper, 19 × 20.8 cm. (7½ × 8¼ in.) New York, Metropolitan Museum of Art, Harris Brisbane Dick Fund

98. Berthe Morisot. *A Summer's Day*. 1879. Oil on canvas, 46 × 75 cm. (18 × 29½ in.) London, National Gallery

market gardeners' patches, quarries and uncanny-looking, tumble-down buildings. As for the Bois de Boulogne itself, it was so ugly by day and so dangerous by night that the less there is to be said about it the better.'

Napoleon III and the landscape architect Adolphe Alphand had transformed the area into a seemingly natural arrangement of winding paths, lakes, and clumps of planting, designed to create the effect of a peaceful rural setting. Everything was contrived to give the sensation of well-being and of rustic charm calculated to appeal to the city dweller (Pl. 93), even though, as one writer commented: 'Apart from the ground and the trees, everything is artificial . . . all that is missing is a mechanical duck'. Charles Marville's photographs (Pl. 94) reinforced this impression of idyllic nature, whose 'artificial beauty', as Gustave Claudin commented, was much to be preferred to 'the repulsive realities of our fields and woods'. The Bois was seen by Parisians as '. . . a place of repose, of pleasures and of health where Paris relaxes her nerves, calms her fevers, refreshes herself, cheers herself . . . It is an Eden where nature and art are married.' Morisot's glimpses of the glades, lakes, avenues, and sheltered enclaves of the Bois give no indication of the contrivance of the setting. Her cut-off compositions evoke an effect of nature observed. While Mallarmé waxed lyrical about the forest of Fontainebleau, and questioned her taste for what he described as 'the moderate groves and mediocre shades' of the Bois, she painted and drew many views of it (Pls. 95, 96, 97, 98), content with what Paul Valéry was to call 'nature's Parisian parsimony'. Residents of other parts of Paris flocked to the park on Sundays to take advantage of its many recreational facilities, walking, running, cycling, ice-skating, horse-racing, or to enjoy the spectacle provided by the lively throngs, but Morisot's view of the Bois de Boulogne was that of a Passy dweller, privileged to enjoy the park at its most tranquil and serene.

Morisot's vision is of nature tamed. Her choice of subjects centres on her immediate surroundings, primarily Paris and its environs. Even when she travelled further afield, it was to places newly connected to Paris by railway and defined, for her, by their relationship to the city. Like the other Impressionists, she preferred the familiar, often the domestic. Frequently she chose to represent her family in the shelter and enclosure of the gardens or that extended garden, the Bois de Boulogne, rather than looking to the overall view or the grand picturesque effect. Her paintings record an intimate and closely observed world, which remained essentially the same despite her frequent changes of scene. For Morisot, the landscape served as a setting for the modest rituals of everyday life.

Bibliography

Books on Berthe Morisot:

M. L. BATAILLE and G. WILDENSTEIN, *Berthe Morisot: Catalogue des peintures, pastels et aquarelles*, Paris, 1961.
DENIS ROUART (ed.), *The Correspondence of Berthe Morisot*, newly introduced and edited by Kathleen Adler and Tamar Garb, London, 1986.
JEAN DOMINIQUE REY, *Berthe Morisot*, Naefels, 1982.

General books on Impressionism and on nineteenth-century women artists:

T. J. CLARK, *The Painting of Modern Life: Paris in the Art of Manet and His Followers*, London, 1985.
TAMAR GARB, *Women Impressionists*, Oxford, 1986.
CHARLES S. MOFFETT *et al.*, *The New Painting: Impressionism 1874–1886*, Oxford, 1986.
JOHN REWALD, *The History of Impressionism*, New York [1946], 1973.
CHARLOTTE ELIZABETH YELDHAM, *Women Artists in Nineteenth-Century England and France*, New York and London, 1984.

Acknowledgements
All quotations of the Morisot correspondence are from Denis Rouart (ed.), *The Correspondence of Berthe Morisot*, newly introduced and edited by Kathleen Adler and Tamar Garb, London, Camden Press, 1986.

We acknowledge our use of the following publications: Janine Bailly-Herzberg, 'Les estampes de Berthe Morisot', *Gazette des Beaux-Arts*, May–June 1979; Richard Bretell, Scott Schaefer, *et al.*, *A Day in the Country*, Los Angeles Museum of Art, 1984; Alain Clairet, ' "Le Cérisier" de Mézy', *L'Oeil*, May 1985; T. J. Clark, *The Painting of Modern Life: Paris in the Art of Manet and His Followers*, London, 1985; Bonnie L. Grad and Timothy A. Riggs, *Visions of City and Country: Prints and Photographs of Nineteenth-Century France*, Worcester Museum of Art, Mass., 1982; Charles S. Moffett *et al.*, *The New Painting: Impressionism 1874–1886*, Oxford, 1986.

Index